SHAKESPEARE'S CHILDREN

Danny Keaney

WITH

DALE LE VACK

ORIGINAL WRITING

© 2012 Danny Keaney and Dale le Vack
Email: dannykeaney@btinternet.com

The right of Danny Keaney and Dale le Vack to be identified as joint authors of this work has been asserted by them in accordance with the Copyright, Designs and Patents Act 1988. First published in the UK in 2012 by Original Writing of Dublin. www.originalwriting.ie

ISBNs:
Parent - 978-1-908282-99-6
ePub - 978-1-908477-45-3
Mobi - 978-1-908477-46-0

All rights reserved.

No part of this publication may be reproduced or transmitted in any form or by any means, electronic or mechanical, including photocopy, recording, or an information storage and retrieval system, without permission in writing from the writer.

A catalogue record for this book is available from the British Library

Book Cover Design Andy Saxby

Photographs reproduced by kind permission of Brenda Dance, Pamela and Ann Keaney, Peter Jones, Martin and Colin Brook, Colin Brook also for his pencil drawings, Olive English, Mrs Phyllis Wren, James Keaney , Jane O' Malley

Photographic reproduction by Fran Freeman

Publisher's Note: Every effort has been made to contact the authors of copyright material reproduced in this volume. Apologies are offered in advance for any unauthorised usage.

Printed by CLONDALKIN GROUP, Glasnevin, Dublin 11

This book is dedicated to my brother Cavan

INTRODUCTION

This book is, I would say, nothing more than a reflection on an uneventful or perhaps an eventful childhood depending on the reader's point of view. It is certainly not an autobiography by any stretch of the imagination and nor is it meant to be. When you get to a certain age and look back over the years that have flown by (as your Granny said it would) then you do start to reflect on life and wonder could it have been different?---the answer to that is yes. Would I have changed mine? Some parts most certainly, but that is the same for most of us. As a child you have no control of what life throws at you up to a certain age and have to take it on the chin--- (literally) in my case— but I wasn't alone. There were many like me in my peer group who have "taken it on the chin" so why would I want to commit my childhood experiences to print? --- quite simple really---I was asked to.

Over the years my old Stratford "muckers" and I have often spoken about the antics we got up to in our childhood in and around the "Shakespeare free" area of Justin's Avenue in Stratford-on- Avon, a place where youngsters from other parts of the town feared for their safety.

Many others will have their own memories of the "Arab camp" in the 50s and how it was for them. I have only scratched the surface of my time as a "camper" and have avoided going any deeper into this once- brutal culture. I can only say it is perhaps for someone else to consider doing that --- before we all curl our toes up. Quite literally there are many things in my memory that I just cannot commit to print. I apologise in advance for the colourful language used---not nice—but it had to go in for reasons of authenticity.

The two most persuasive people who literally twisted my arm to get the pen out and dust it down were John Evans, brother of "Studger" who you will read about later and his wife Beverley of the Wareing family, who lived in Woodlands Road; both good old "salt of the earth" Stratford families.

I for one found it a very testing time in my formative years to be thrown into a severe alien environment, not helped by disinterested parents and fed to the wolves, where you had to learn the lesson of looking after yourself at the school of hard knocks as quickly as you could.

Believe me, being brought up in and around the Arab camp area of Stratford as a young child fresh from being molly-coddled by doting grandparents in rural Norfolk was a frightening experience, especially for people like me who were at the bottom of the food-chain. It was not good. The austere world of the 50s where the only colour seemed to be grey and most people depressed at the thought of the long struggle ahead after the war years, all added to the negative thoughts in my head about this hell I had been thrown into.

Most parents up the camp would not have known about the fights between their children, some very serious and could have quite easily resulted in a death on occasions. There were many decent families with sensible children who had no interest in the regular and gratuitous violence going on around them and the petty thieving, mainly from Mrs. Jessop's shop: she that sold meat that had seen better days, but people still bought it and were grateful. Mrs Jessop and her husband George needed to have eyes in the back of their head when all the scruffy little urchins with their arse hanging out of their trousers, grazed knees and black eyes turned up at their shop hungry for sweets — but no money.

I remember Mrs. Jessop with great affection. She was always expensively attired on her days off, resplendent in her fur coat, and hers was a name synonymous with Justin's Avenue of the 1950s. Ah, Mrs. Jessop---they don't make them like her any more.

Then there was the bread-man's horse that used to stop at the right house without being told so that the bread-man could deliver his proper loaf of bread to the specific order of the house. He told us that his horse was "bomb-proof" and "rock-steady". He really shouldn't have said that because a penny banger was let off beside man and horse and it ended up with the horse bolting for about 20 yards. The loaves were thrown off the back of his cart all over the road, where greedy little hands were waiting to carry them off.

There was a very hard edge to life on estates like ours in Stratford, but all of us kids were sufficiently aware of our nationality and pride in being British to stand to attention for one minute on the strike of eleven o'clock every year on Remembrance Day and we used to know it as 11/11/11 - the eleventh hour of the eleventh day of the eleventh month.

Kids would wait excitedly for the moment to come, no adults in sight, and stand to attention for one minute. Something we didn't have to be told to do was to show respect for those who had fought for our freedom. We lived among Second World War veterans such as Bill Sparrow, Vic Whistler, "Pip" Troughton, Arthur Smith and Harold (Joe) Pitts.

Some had fought in Normandy, some had fought in Africa with "Monty" and up through Italy at the "sharp end." There were many more. They might not have known it but we "snotty nosed" little kids knew of them and admired them---still do.

Yes it was tough, most of the kids from the "camp" area in the 50s and 60s could tell a similar story; of the slaps, the punches, the knees to the groin, taken and given, of the "scratting" around looking for empty pop-bottles to take to the shop in exchange for a few pence, the ration books, the rag and bone man who would give you a "day old" chick for a few items of threadbare clothing, dogs humping on street corners, the gas street-lights that would "pop on" as dusk fell, sugar sandwiches, the seemingly long and snowy winters which made you shiver in your cold house, some dads dragging branches down Justin's Avenue hill that they had lopped off trees on the Clopton Estate to make fires to warm their 'frozen' kids.

All this was going on in the beautiful and genteel town of Stratford-upon-Avon, where the well heeled people went about their business unconcerned about "them up that end," and where in another part of town some of the most famous actors and actresses of the day strutted their stuff on the stage of the Memorial Theatre - to applause from "the toffs".

Yes, the Stratford "bourgeois elite" knew of us, the ruffians who sometimes gave their children a slap. I can imagine them mentioning the "Arab campers" in hushed tones only.

Anyone in my peer group could have written a similar story to mine, or indeed anyone of my age, but I found it very time consuming and often struggled for inspiration. That was where my collaborator Dale le Vack came in. He was absolutely brilliant. He would grab me metaphorically by the scruff of the neck and say "just get on with it you lazy sod" --- so I did ---thanks Dale.

I have gone off at a bit of a tangent with the sections on Norfolk and Ireland, but my story couldn't just be about Stratford and Justin's Avenue as intended. There has to be a beginning and a conclusion in later life that is linked to ancestry and upbringing. If anything, this book has helped me to discover who I really am, as the reader will discover when I introduce my third cousin Sean McDermott (MacDiarmada) recently described in the title of a book about him as The Mind of the Revolution in Dublin in 1916.

They say I was a tearaway later in my youth and I probably was at times, but I can put my hand on my heart when I say that none of us, with very few exceptions, ever set out to cause hurt to people or to live on the wrong side of the law. Unfortunately, perhaps, a few myths and legends have grown up over the years which are not entirely accurate.

I was no angel but after the age of 17, when I returned for the last time from Norfolk to live in Stratford, I had made up my mind that I would never again be the victim of bullying or gratuitous violence. Anyone who tried it on with me would get it without hesitation and this resulted in many scrapes; none of which I am ashamed of being involved in.

Nevertheless, I suppose some of us in our adolescent years of the 1960s acquired a reputation for being "hard" boys from the wrong side of the track; the fact is although we got locked up by the police on many occasions, we had a respect for the law (and felt it too sometimes with a good cuffing from the men in blue). All of us have grown up to be exceptionally law abiding citizens and in many cases successful businessmen.

In my case the most important and influential person in my life has been my wife Lorraine, who came from a very good family and must at first have been nonplussed by my arrival in her life.

She has steadied me and tolerated my occasional excesses to an astonishing degree, tolerant of my years as a pro- hunt activist and intimidator of bus drivers (sorry John McKenna) when the tourist buses got out of hand in Stratford.

I'd like to say thank you to Lorraine for 40 years of wonderful marriage - and thanks also to my son Justin for being such an understanding sort. Some people are still amused that a proficient football referee should have been spawned by a bloke who got banned twice from playing rugby for life.

I have a list of people I should like to thank for helping me to make this book possible:Pat Bambridge for resisting the temptation to tell me to clear off when she really should have done. My persistent questioning concerning the workings of a contraption called a computer and its printer must have driven Pat to drink. Pat, a caring Christian lady with a very sweet demeanour, must have pulled her hair out at times—Oh how I tested her patience as I did her fellow computer experts Margaret and Gaynor. The lovely mad and scatty Fran Freeman for her invaluable and very professional photographic assistance---good fun is Fran but she always gets the job done.

Thanks to Olive English for her encouragement. I should like to say a special thank you to Sir Arnold Wesker for allowing me to use his "Angry Poem." It is a very personal poem of Sir Arnold's and I feel highly honoured. Then there is Derrick Smart, a "good old Justin's boy," who took the time to remind me of a couple of "gems." Thanks to Rachel Dale for her suggestion to include in the book, a map of Stratford.

Finally I should like to thank local historian, author and playwright Steve Newman for writing the foreword to my book because although I did not know him at Hugh Clopton Secondary School, he was also a victim of its often brutish culture and perhaps unlike me overcame its educational shortcomings to prove that we weren't all thick.

He also introduces the intriguing aspect of the parallel universe that existed in the 20th century in the form of the "haves" who went to see Shakespeare performed at the Theatre and the "have nots" to whom a performance was going to the Picture House on a Saturday morning and a fight with the "posh" kids from Maidenhead Road. Steve, you've done me proud and helped to underline that me – and many others – are perhaps the true children of the old Bard.

Danny Keaney

Contents

Introduction vii
by *Danny Keaney*

Foreword xvii
by *Steve Newman*

Chapter One
THE NORFOLK POACHER 1

Chapter Two
A DYSFUNCTIONAL FAMILY 38

Chapter Three
AT SCHOOL IN STRATFORD 54

Chapter Four
THE ARAB CAMP 83

Chapter Five
THE MAN WITH A GUN IN A TREE 106

Chapter Six
THE BATTLE OF WILLS 115

Chapter Seven
A FAMOUS IRISH RELATIVE 146

Chapter Eight
A REBEL AGAIN 176

Foreword

Steve Newman - Bachelor of Arts (Hons) History
*Hugh Clopton Secondary Modern School,
Stratford-upon-Avon 1959-62*

When I was asked to write a foreword for *Shakespeare's Children* and give it an historical perspective I was both delighted and terrified. I knew nothing about Danny, or the book for that matter, but meeting Danny and reading the extraordinary account of his life in both Stratford and Norfolk, I simply couldn't resist. I hope I do him and his book justice by using the history of the town, and most especially Shakespeare and the town's theatres, as something of a counter-weight to Danny's own dramatic, funny and delightful story *Shakespeare's Children*.

Stratford-upon-Avon has many sides to its character. It's a beautiful and ancient town by the river that has attracted millions of visitors for centuries, but was also, until quite recently, a centre for livestock sales and slaughter - where the gutters quite literally ran with blood, even until the 1960s. From 1837 to 1967 it was also the home of Flowers Brewery, which employed over 3,000 local people, more than 10% of the town's population back in the 1950s.

Of course, it's also the birthplace and resting place of William Shakespeare and, since the late 1870s, the home of several theatres dedicated to his memory, the first built by Charles Edward Flower. The town has also been a centre for Christian worship for over twelve-hundred years, with Holy Trinity Church (Shakespeare's Church) founded in 1210.

By the end of the 18th century Stratford was also a hub of the canal network and until Dr Beeching wielded his axe in the 1960s it stood at the heart of the rail network, which enabled it to become a regional centre for light industry and food distribution. This early transport infrastructure helped to sustain a thriving retail industry, including some of the country's first department stores.

By 1924 the town had over thirty road transport and bus companies, in excess of 400 private businesses, eight places of worship, six schools, one newspaper, five world class hotels, scores of off-licences, plus over twenty pubs in the town centre, none of which, until the outbreak of the First World War, was governed by any licensing laws.

Consequently Shakespeare's Stratford has never been a quaint, dreamy market town, but a rather noisy and rough town. This atmosphere features in just about every play that Shakespeare wrote. The drunken swordplay may be set in Verona, but the place Shakespeare was thinking about as he scratched away with his quill was 16th century Stratford in the early hours of a Saturday or Sunday morning. Nothing has changed.

Until academia took Shakespeare to its bosom toward the end of the 19th century, Stratford had been quite happy with its place in the scheme of things. It worked hard, worshipped and drank well – or extolled the virtues of abstinence - enjoyed its markets and two annual Mop Fairs. It was also quite proud of Shakespeare, especially as it meant another knees-up on the 23rd of April each year, thanks to David Garrick's invention of the

Shakespeare Birthday Celebrations in 1769. Hundreds of people thronged the sixpenny standing area of the new 1879 theatre to enjoy Barry Sullivan's - and later Frank Benson's - spectacular productions, especially during the so called 'Golden Era' from the 1890s to the outbreak of World War One.

Of course, the majority of Stratford's population, as now, never gave Shakespeare, or the new theatre, a thought - although a growing number did begin to wonder what all the fuss was about.

Some even considered that Charles Flower should have spent his money on improving the living conditions of the poor, who in the 1870s and 1880s existed in mean conditions within a stone's throw of the new theatre.

Consequently, a growing resentment began to boil over, expressing itself in vandalism. In the early 1880s a group of youngsters wrecked the theatre gardens; and to such an extent they were fenced-off for a couple of years, which, of course, created even more resentment. As William Shakespeare became an icon for the academic establishment, including the governors of his school, who had kept him very much at arm's length until then, the split began to open up on a national and local scale. The lines were drawn between those who might have considered themselves to be the natural descendants of Shakespeare, Shakespeare's Children if you will, and those who they perceived were now taking him away from them.

Suddenly the Bard was no longer the 'people's poet' but a member, albeit in death, of the establishment, one of the powerful. He may even have been thought of as an oppressor by many when his work became part of the national curriculum at around the same time, which, often through atrocious teaching, created, for many – including Danny – an indifference to William Shakespeare and his work.

In the September of 1959 Hugh Clopton Secondary Modern School felt more like a German Prisoner of War Camp than a place of education. All we could expect was brutality and bad food. On that first day of term – it must have been the same for Danny in 1958 - we were lined up in our grey blazers and short grey trousers ready for inspection by the Herr Kommandant, who looked like a bad imitation of the 1930s film star Will Hay. This was Will Hay with a difference. Gone were the befuddled attitude, askew spectacles, and inherent kindness. Peter Fred Kite Sellers – the deputy headmaster - walked down the ranks whacking each boy on the back of the legs with his cane.

Thwack!

"I shall turn you into men who respect authority."

Thwack! Smack!

We were at the mercy of men who'd had, one way or another, a pretty rough time during the war, or were just vindictive sods who'd inherited corporal punishment as the only means to keep us quiet. One of them taught chemistry and loved to take out his considerable anger on the boys with a T-square. It didn't take much to make him angry. A cough at the wrong moment and he'd give the offender a going over with the blunt end of the aforementioned technical drawing implement. I don't think any of us got away without a dose of that remedy for perceived indiscipline, certainly not me or, I suspect, Danny.

One day we decided to teach him a lesson. The chemistry teacher had taught us that the element phosphorus, at least I think it was phosphorus, once taken out of water, will smoulder and eventually burn in oxygen. He'd shown us some very smelly experiments. One day when he'd left the classroom to discuss that afternoon's football fixture, a couple of us unlocked the chemical storeroom and emptied the water out of two jars containing sticks of phosphorus. We then relocked the storeroom door, putting the key we'd taken from the teacher's coat pocket into his desk drawer, and returned to our desks.

Within minutes smoke was billowing from under the storeroom door, followed a few minutes later by a very flustered chemistry teacher, who couldn't find his keys, desperately trying to break down the storeroom door.

It wasn't a real fire, just a lot of very smelly smoke. No one was ever blamed, but he never used that T-square again.

Danny of course was preoccupied with violence at school – not only at Hugh Clopton but at Stratford's Roman Catholic School which he describes in detail in *Shakespeare's Children* – and the violence around Justin's Avenue that had created a sub-culture of brutish and mindless behaviour that became inherent if you lived in certain parts of Stratford.

If you were unlucky enough not to find a way out early then this sub-culture of violence could easily become a part of your adult make-up, unless you found something, or someone, to ease you away from the violence and petty crime.

At Hugh Clopton Secondary Modern I witnessed all this but was not strong enough to confront it, so frequently I made my way after school to the theatre, not because I'd suddenly found a love for Shakespeare, but because I wanted to be close to what had, for me, become something of a shrine; somewhere where you might bump into one of the young hell-raising actors such as Peter O'Toole or Albert Finney.

It was the one place in Stratford where I felt I was a part of the new order, where – had you been encouraged to discover books as I was - you could read D.H. Lawrence, Dickens, Hemingway and Whitman, or Ian Fleming.

Suddenly theatre and the new British cinema with young British actors portraying young men like Danny-think of *Saturday Night and Sunday Morning* - were at last coming together for the very first time. Suddenly in the early 1960s everything seemed 'real', with that line between culture and resentment at last dissolving, at least for me. It was all down to one man.

When Peter Hall took over the Shakespeare Memorial Theatre in 1960 he was no stranger to Stratford. The first British director of Beckett's *Waiting for Godot* had first visited Stratford as a 16 year old in 1946, when he'd cycled the 120 miles from his Suffolk home to see a production of Peter Brook's *Love's Labour's Lost*.

Twelve years later, in 1958, he was back again, but this time he was not in the audience but directing a very young Geraldine McEwan in *Twelfth Night*. A year later he was directing Laurence Olivier in *Coriolanus*, and Charles Laughton in *King Lear*, and a member of Frank Benson's 1913 company, Dame Edith Evans, as Volumnia. Although not directed by Hall, that season also saw Paul Robeson's mighty Othello – and I did get to meet him -with Sam Wanamaker as Iago.

The railway worker's son from Suffolk was mixing in the right company and couldn't put a foot wrong. Had he not had aspiring parents and gone to Cambridge when he did, he might have been a rebel like Danny. What Peter Hall did on taking over the

Memorial Theatre from Glen Byam Shaw was get rid of the so-called star system and start making new stars out of young actors such as the aforementioned Peter O'Toole and Albert Finney, Ian Holm, Edward Woodward, Dorothy Tutin, Richard Johnson, and Geraldine McEwan.

He also started a regime of intellectual stimulation by employing John Barton to explain to the actors the nature of Shakespeare's texts, and how they should be spoken. He employed that most determined of directors, Peter Brook, to ensure that some exciting new productions would soon put Stratford back on the map, most notably *A Midsummer's Night Dream*, and Shakespeare's 'History' cycle of plays. Most surprisingly he demanded that the name of the theatre be changed to the Royal Shakespeare Theatre (RST), and that an acting company be created called the Royal Shakespeare Company (RSC), and that to be able to do this, and see his ambitious artistic plans fulfilled, Hall must have state funding.

The first Arts Council grant to the RSC was around £125,000, a huge sum nearly fifty years ago, which went up year by year, with the RSC and the National Theatre fighting ever since over funds. By the end of Hall's reign the RST was a much more open and welcoming place: gone was the somewhat snooty atmosphere that still prevailed there during Anthony Quayle's tenure. Peter Hall changed that, as did his successors Trevor Nunn and Adrian Noble, as do Michael Boyd and Gregory Doran to this day.

When the idea of the Courtyard Theatre, built on the car park of The Other Place, which was itself the site of the temporary 1864 theatre, was first suggested, there was a letter in *The Stratford Herald* asking why the RSC couldn't use an old warehouse space they already owned and had used twenty years earlier as a theatre.

The reason it wasn't used is because it was a dreadful place. It was considered rather daring and innovative to have a play, *Mary, After the Queen*, which was about local people, acted out in the rusty, echoing old brewery warehouse where the actors, including the formidable Peggy Mount, had to shout every line to make themselves heard. They were competing with the din of at least a thousand starlings calling to each other on the roof. Verisimilitude it was not. I have my doubts if the writer of that *Herald* letter had actually seen a performance there

It was dire, it was dirty, with interval drinks available from a couple of vending machines, but it was a space that was seen as hugely significant as something of a working-class protest against Maggie Thatcher and her regime; and in the 1980s the RSC was on something of a mission to give Maggie a bashing.

The project at The Other Place was conceived after Angela Hewins wrote her book, *The Dillen*, about George Hewins, her husband's grandfather. George was one of Stratford's many characters considered by most who met him to be a foul-mouthed old devil. I only ever spoke to him once back in the 1960s. He was walking toward me with the use of a zimmer frame, and as we passed he grabbed my left arm in a vice-like grip and growled:

"What's the time, old man?" (I jest - he was much more succinct).

"Ten thirty," I replied. With that he spat on the pavement and told me to go forth and multiply, using fewer words and then shuffled off. Angela's book is a superb piece of social history, and beautifully written, although you won't find George using any foul language. It was inevitable that the RSC, then run by the fearless Trevor Nunn, would see *The Dillen*, with George portrayed as something of a working-class rebel, as ideal material with which to clobber Maggie Thatcher. The book was quickly turned into a play by Angela Hewins and the RSC's writer in residence at the time, Ron Hutchinson, with direction by Barry Kyle.

It was produced in 1983 as a promenade piece that kicked-off at The Other Place, before marching around the town acting out scenes on several relevant street corners, again with Peggy Mount, before ending-up back at The Other Place. It was hugely successful, and perhaps for the first time many Stratford people were able to access their own theatre company and feel part of the action on those street corners, including several newer versions of George Hewins, who made their own very colourful, and very verbal contributions.

Mary, AfterThe Queen, Angela Hewins' sequel to *The Dillen*, was a book about the lives of George Hewins' children, especially their working lives at the canning factory on the Birmingham Road, just down from Justin's Avenue where Danny lived. The book was less of a success, but like its predecessor it was quickly turned into a play by the same team.Anyway, that sort of stuff has never really been tried since.

Poor old George Hewins was feted for a bit before he died, having his photo taken backstage at the theatre and shaking hands with the mayor, and no doubt asking him the 'effing time too. In fact George had had his theatrical day back in 1912 when he was one of Frank Benson's 'supers' for a season, earning between sixpence and a shilling for each performance, which was quite a lot for a builder's labourer who only earned two shillings for a ten hour day. Apparently Benson liked George because he thought he looked a bit like Shakespeare and may easily have been a descendant of one of the Bard's many bastard children.

Danny Keaney and George Hewins are linked socially and emotionally. The social split is personified in George and his family, with Danny something of an inheritor. In George's day the poor lived in the centre of Stratford in the many Courts that burrowed away from the main streets close to the slaughter houses. Their plight was known by all, not least Councillor Justin who owned and ran the Shakespeare Hotel. She was, apart from being an excellent business woman, a caring and thoughtful person who left strict instructions for her chef to feed the hungry kids and their families who lived in the small cottages bordering the back of the hotel, close to what had once been Shakespeare's garden.

This altruism brought her many friends and encouraged many of the actors who stayed in her hotel for the short festival season to follow her lead by giving food and money to many of the same families, at the same time encouraging them to come to the theatre and acquaint themselves with Shakespeare. Ironically, when Justin's Avenue, named after the philanthropic hotelier Councillor Justin, and the surrounding streets were built between the wars, it meant that the highly visible poverty problem that had been so apparent, and embarrassing with overseas tourists around, was now out of the sight of the great and good of the town and pretty much out of mind.

So the split reappeared. George Hewins and his family ended up living in the same area as Danny, whereas George had been born and brought up in the town centre. In World War Two the available factory work lifted the less fortunate out of poverty, brought in more immigrants and kept them in work, if not out of trouble. Stratford, as I have said, was a rowdy town. By the time Danny came along he found himself pushed from pillar to post, the subject of brutal treatment at school and as an adolescent not infrequently in brushes with the law. Only Danny's strength of character and good humour would eventually set him on the right road. Danny's story, *Shakespeare's Children,* is not another victim's memoir – Danny was never a victim – but an uplifting, funny and in the end spiritual tale from which we can all learn. It contributes strongly to Stratford's 20th century history and should be regarded in that context as an important piece of work. Danny's later life as one of Warwickshire's 'in your face' pro-hunt activists in the early years of the millennium and the reader's introduction to his famous kinsman Sean McDermott, executed after the 1916 Easter Monday Uprising in Dublin, also give us a clearer insight into Danny's rebellious nature.

Born in Wellesbourne in 1947, the same year as Danny, Steve Newman has spent nearly fifty years working in the retail industry. He joined the independent Stratford store Fred Winter Ltd in 1998. Since the late 1980s Steve has also been a professional writer and playwright, with plays produced in Stratford, London, Oxford, Birmingham and Edinburgh. When not writing he is also an actor and director. Living in Stratford with his wife Hilary, Steve - a committed Christian - is also an historian with an honours degree in the humanities and history. Steve attended Stratford's Hugh Clopton Secondary Modern School but worked for his degree long after he had left the school.

Shakespeare's Children

Chapter One

THE NORFOLK POACHER

"Yet this is a lovely land. The summers are warm, the winters mild. Game is abundant, and the soils are easily cultivated. What more can a tribe, seeking a place to settle, ask for? This is a good place to call home."

Ralph Whitlock (Guardian columnist and author)

The dark-eyed boy walked furtively down the country lane looking for the hollow tree. It was a secret the boy had shared with the old man since he was not much more than a toddler – he would never divulge the hiding place of the family gun to a living soul.

Charlie Baker was a quiet man, not given to talking to others about his business, although everyone in the village knew he was a poacher. Now, lung cancer had taken the chain-smoking Charlie down to skin and bone in just a few months – the funeral had been held the day before and he was interred in the churchyard of St Mary the Virgin. It was the autumn of 1958.

Charlie's grandson was the sole keeper of the gun secret and he presumed without question it was he who should inherit the firearm that the old man had left in the tree. He had, after all, been Fafa's sole companion as a poacher for several years. The ancient Belgian single-barrel shotgun was his by right.

The gun must have been nearly 100 years old and it was lethal, with a pitted and rusted barrel that made it highly dangerous to fire. The boy did not know that, neither did he wonder at the time why an old soldier (16856 Private C. Baker 7th Battalion Norfolk Regiment), who must have been aware of the importance of keeping a gun in good and clean condition, had kept his personal firearm in such a dangerous state.

The hollow ash, covered in ivy, was less than half a mile outside the south Norfolk village of Saxlingham Nethergate, along a sunken lane, and the boy looked around him to make sure he had not been followed before stepping up to the tree and reaching down into the darkness.

He felt the familiar damp jute sack and the three rigid components within it before pulling the bundle out of the hollow and exposing it to the daylight. It was then he remembered the last poaching expedition they'd been on the previous year when the grey partridge were jugging up (sleeping) in the stubble in late September.

Wild grey partridge had been abundant in those years in East Anglia and it was not unusual to have 20 coveys, of more than two dozen birds each, on a farm of 200 acres. Each covey would roost on the stubble at night – until the field was ploughed in the New Year - grouped closely together and on alert for predators.

The tightly-packed birds would leave shit and feathers in the circle where they'd jugged up the night before, so it was not difficult for Charlie to deduce where they would be congregating the next night.

There was nothing sporting in the way they were shot. The poacher would just blast the covey from close range, killing as many as he could, "shooting into the brown" the old poachers called it. With luck, he might take six or seven birds.

The junior poacher...

"Blast you bor," said Fafa to me as my almost imperceptible movement in the hedge behind him disturbed the covey of 30 partridge. They had come to roost that evening only 25 yards away in the stubble of Farmer Simmons' biggest arable field, moving nervously across the ground to the spot where Fafa knew by instinct they would jug up until daybreak.

I could almost hear my heart beating in the silence as they edged closer to us, anticipating the moment Charlie would open fire when they had bunched up close to each other. The single rusty barrel of his 12-bore shotgun was trained on the covey. My arse was aching and my right leg had gone numb.

He was about to pull the trigger, a lit Woodbine perched on his lower lip, when I shifted my feet. The partridge sensed the movement and flew off, calling out in high-pitched fright, darting in demented arcs a few feet off the ground, to the sanctuary of the next field.

The old man stood up and lifted the battered trilby off his head, throwing it to the ground in mock irritation, as if to stamp on it. He had a broad Norfolk sense of humour and I loved him dearly.

He always wore an ex-army leather jerkin over a mud-stained heavy coat, with the sleeves pulled slightly up his forearms, exposing enormous hands. The trilby was on his head, whatever the weather.

"Blast you bor," he repeated in his broad Norfolk accent, this time with a smile. Fafa always forgave me if I made some kind of fidgety movement which put the birds up. Partridge shooting demanded complete self-discipline. The stalker had to stay absolutely still, sometimes for as long as half an hour, waiting for the covey to approach. It could be agonisingly painful, but the slightest movement of hand or foot would set off the partridge in fright, because they were alert for predators such as foxes, weasels and stoats.

As a veteran of the 1914-18 War he told me how he would lie motionless in the mud, rifle in hand, waiting for movement above the enemy trenches, then 'shoot them in the napper'...those partridges wouldn't have stood a chance if I hadn't been with him. My lovely gentle grandfather had killed another human being in cold-blood, but war brutalizes and being a soldier it was his job to kill.

I had known partridge would be there of an evening, because I had seen them coming to roost on the exact spot the day before. I stood motionless under the oak tree in the playground of the village school, watching the partridge shuffling nervously towards the far corner of the stubble field to jug up for the night.

I had just done detention for yet another transgression of the head teacher's rule book. Most of the 30 children at the school behaved better than I did. When I got back to the cottage, where grandmother Nellie was waiting with our tea, Fafa, a wiry man of average height with many thousands of hours of agricultural labouring work engrained on his weather-beaten face, said we would net some partridge the following evening.

I did very little school work the next day and spent most of it gazing out of the window at the field where we would stalk the birds that night.

"Pay attention Danny Keaney," the teacher ordered sternly more than once.

I much preferred going out in the evening with Fafa to getting up before dawn in the freezing cold and walking quietly under the canopy of a starlit sky behind him. We would trudge across the frosty fields to a hide, or to check his snares. I'd always be there, mind you, whatever the time he left the cottage.

He never had to wake me up. We'd have a quick cup of tea, a wash with cold water and be off into the dark to pick up his gun from the hollow tree in the lane.

"Sorry Fafa," I mumbled as we trudged after the partridge debacle across the field to the village and the comfort of the Prince of Wales run by 'Nibby', a man of great character and full of bullshit. After concealing his rusty gun carefully in the hollow tree, Charlie imbibed a couple of frothy pints of Bullards bitter. I remained outside in the cart shed with a bottle of Vimto and a packet of Smith's crisps, the ones with the little blue salt packet.

In a small shed he kept a very long and rather heavy net of about one inch mesh, 20 yards across and 10 yards deep. It took two strong men to operate the net effectively and that night we took Charlie's brother Wicket. (I've no idea why he was called that). Charlie was on one end and his brother on the other. I waited from a few yards away, because I wasn't tall or strong enough to hold the net up and cover the distance required at netting pace.

Netting required strength, endurance and stealth. They had to hold it very tight and drag it at a height of about four feet over the stubble, until they were on the covey. Then they'd drop the net fast. It would fall heavily on the bewildered partridges, trapping them in the mesh. You could hear the terrified birds several fields away. The secret was to anticipate exactly where the birds were jugging up and in Charlie's case it was his instinct and years of experience. It was my job to jump on the net and kill as many as I could.

"Go on bor, get on 'em quick," Charlie and Wicket shouted at me.

We took nearly 20 partridge that night and were well pleased. The birds were, and still are, regarded as a delicacy. I dived on the net and grabbed as many birds as I could, wringing their neck with practiced ease.

It was exciting stuff.

I idolised my grandfather Charlie Baker. Up to my reaching the age of 11, when the old man died at the age of 67, everything I knew about the countryside came from him. He worked hard, perhaps 10 hours a day, and more at harvest time, but he always had time in his life for reflection and a little conversation despite the hours of toil.

Such was the pace in mid-1950s Saxlingham Nethergate and had been for generations. The agricultural way of life meant the clock ticked slowly. If a car came through the village we'd all stop what we were doing and stare at it. We Norfolk car starers must have looked a strange bloody lot to the driver of the car—big ones, little ones, all staring---scary.

The noises of the world for us were the hammering of the blacksmith's anvil at the forge, the sound of a tractor in a nearby field, human voices calling cows in the fields and birdsong in the spring and summer. There was no traffic noise from the A140 Norwich-Ipswich road a mile or so away.

It was Charlie's job to bury the contents of the family soil bucket every week, and one of my all-abiding memories is of him going up the village street carrying a bucket of human excrement and greeting somebody coming the other way doing the same.

They stopped at the side of the road, each putting down his bucket of shit, lit two Woodbines and had a conversation. It still amuses me, but that was normal village life in Norfolk in those days. That bucket and its contents would have made a great 'still life' painting in hindsight, with the various shades of brown rising to a peak and glistening in that "special" Norfolk light which the Norwich school of artists often spoke of; it would have looked a treat hanging on the wall of the Tate Modern along with the other crap that finds a home there these days.

It seemed normal being without a flush toilet at home and before I went to Stratford at the age of five I'd never used one. If the chamber pot under the bed was used to have a pee during the night, we were told not to put it back immediately but wait, because my grandfather believed that the steam would make the springs go rusty. That was taken in all seriousness and probably had some truth behind it. There have certainly been a lot of changes to my way of life in 60 years.

Life on the farm...

Horses were still used on some farms and I have snapshots in my mind from a very young age of muck carting, carting the hay and the corn, watching Fafa plough the fields, and sitting on the back of the cart dropping off mangolds to the livestock in the cold winter months after Christmas.

Fafa was in charge of the two shire horses on the tenant farm rented by Fred English and sometimes, in the summer, I would be allowed to ride the foal bareback, when the horses were put into the low meadows to graze and kept out overnight.

At other times of the year, at the end of the day, Charlie would rub the horses down in the farmyard and feed them before leading them into clean stables for the night. When I was about five, I fell off the foal one evening as she was being led to the stable and I remember what seemed like a huge hoof stamping the ground close to my head. If she had kicked me her hoof would have cracked open my skull like an egg. The nearest hospital in Norwich was nearly 10 miles away and my short life would have been over. Some would say an opportunity missed!

As I grew older Fafa and I became inseparable when I wasn't in school. There were not many children of my age in the village at that time and so all my attention was directed towards the farm, helping out where I could, and of course going poaching with the old man.

I mastered the three 'Rs' but spent most hours in the classroom thinking and dreaming about what was going on at the farm. The teachers were not strict or vindictive at the village school in Norfolk, as they were at St Gregory's Roman Catholic School in Stratford-upon-Avon.

When the teachers let us out in the afternoon I'd sprint off to the farm to find Fafa. There was milking to be done in the mid-afternoon through the year and he might be in the milk-shed with the dairy-maid Freda English, or the cowman Ron Day, or mucking out, repairing fences, or digging ditches.

"Whatyer bor!" he would say when I turned up.

In January grandfather would be cutting kale, harvesting sugar beet, harvesting and clamping mangolds for cattle food and looking after the fatstock. Then in the spring, I'd find grandfather sowing corn behind the horses, but never driving the old Massey Ferguson tractor or any other mechanised vehicle. A few months later he'd be hay-making.

Whatever he was doing there would be a Woodbine hanging out of his mouth. They were called 'coffin nails', which in my grandfather's case was grimly accurate. He was to suffer because of those little packets of pleasure, which he would have relied upon to relieve the tension in his days in the World War One trenches, waiting for the next bombardment.

Then in late summer it was harvest-time. Farmer Fred English, armed with his double-barrelled shotgun, knocked off the rabbits which tried to escape in panic from the ever-decreasing cover of the corn as the binder worked the field. You'd have to hop around a bit, because old Fred didn't really care where he aimed his gun if he was following a rabbit.

The cows were brought in for the winter in early December and kept in the sheds until mid-March, but still had to be milked by hand twice a day. Despite what the poet Ralph Whitlock wrote, the winters were hard in Norfolk.

Charlie didn't have a gun, as we know, because it was hidden in the ash tree, but was so quick he could kill the rabbits with a stick. He'd see one trying to hide just inside the corn and with one swipe he could kill it stone dead.

He'd gut the rabbit on the field – you should gut a rabbit almost immediately as opposed to a hare whose flavour improves if it is hung without being gutted – then he'd take home the dead creature and hang it in the larder with all the other game. Fafa was never short of a few rabbits and hares.

Later, my grandfather was part of the team thrashing the corn stacks. A traction engine and steam-powered threshing machine, owned by contractors, used to come to the farm in the autumn, when a smoky smell of burning rotted vegetation was in the air. They'd put wire netting round the stacks, so the rats couldn't get away from the terriers owned by 'Charlo' English, the farmer's son--- terriers and village kids with sticks in hand killing the fleeing rats ---complete mayhem---I loved mayhem.

In the months up to Christmas we'd be sugar-beeting again, or cutting back hedges in the biting cold wind blowing up from the North Sea. There would be half an hour for lunch and most days Charlie would sit in the hedge and cut up some cheese, with his penknife, to eat with a couple of hunks of bread that Nellie had given him.

He would never have thought to complain about the cold because he had grown up in difficult times for people in farming between the wars when manual jobs became scarce because of mechanisation. He felt lucky to have a job.

Later in the afternoon, as his day was coming to an end, he'd be listening for cock pheasants going to roost and he'd make a mental note of which tree they had chosen. That night he'd creep under the tree and shoot them.

Those were times before new intensive farming methods ended the days of the small and traditional enclosed Norfolk field. Ancient hedges were uprooted in the 1970s to create a prairie-type environment, stripping the landscape of much of its wildlife.

Cattle disappeared and the emphasis changed to large-scale cereal production.

Our squire had been against radical change and to his credit kept rents low enough for his tenants to sustain mixed farming for a few more years, thus retaining the hedge-bottoms for the pheasants and partridges to build a nest in concealment. Thousands of rabbits found sanctuary there too.

He also encouraged his tenants not to use large volumes of pesticide and chemical fertilisers, which in the 1950s and 1960s were the other main destroyer of wildlife because they killed the insects lower down the food chain.

Charlie Baker would have hated the changes in agricultural practices, and I'm glad he did not live to see his beloved small fields disappear and their large hedges uprooted in the move towards modernisation and big profits.

He had been a poacher all of his life and was the son and grandson of a poacher. Apart from wartime service in Flanders, as a sniper, he knew only his corner of Norfolk.

He sustained a gunshot wound to his shoulder and was sent back to England, where he was treated for a few weeks at a military hospital in Eastbourne. He had soon recovered and was sent back by troopship to the Western Front in time to play a part in the Battle of Cambrai in 1917, when tanks were used for the first time in support of the infantry. Within two months of returning to France he was posted missing, presumed dead.

In fact he had been captured and spent the rest of the war in Dulmen prisoner-of-war camp in Germany, not far from the Dutch border. He must have missed his Norfolk village and its small fields and woodland, with its abundant wild populations of rabbit, hare, pheasant, partridge and duck. Only the Red Cross parcels kept the prisoners from starving.

Fifty years after Charlie's death, the vast preponderance of game birds in Norfolk are reared. However, thanks to EU set-aside, moves are gradually being made to conserve margins around the fields to give wild birds a chance to breed, but the real Norfolk hedges as they were in Charlie's day will never be replanted.

Charlie pitted himself against truly wild birds that were alert and canny. Their reared descendants offer poor comparison. French partridges, for example, found on many posh shoots these days, are particularly stupid.

Fafa's concession to urban life was a bi-monthly trip to Norwich market to sell the rabbits he reared in the hutches on his allotment. His lifetime - from 1891 to 1958 - witnessed a vanishing world. It had started before the age of motor transport and ended shortly after the Russians launched Sputnik into space.

All seven of the Baker brothers had been poachers at one level or another and the most prolific were Charlie and his brothers Jimson and Sonny. They always had a good supply of game in the larder at their respective cottages, from which they could supplement the wages of a farm labourer.

Sonny, a larger than life character, was regarded as 'a wrong-un'. He was someone who could lay his hands on anything, including fresh meat if the price was right. He sold large quantities of poached game around the district and may have been part of an organised gang of poachers.

It is said he had been on the wrong side of the law on a few occasions, selling contraband tobacco, and was even rumoured to have been a smuggler in his younger days. The police turned up to raid his cottage one day, looking for tobacco, but couldn't locate the contraband it because he'd buried it in the chicken run. His theory was that no 'sniffer' dog could find it through the stink of chicken shit.

When he got older and was retired, he went on trying to rip off people by selling rabbit hutches to London couples who, by then, were beginning to buy houses in Norfolk, many for weekend getaways. He put up a sign outside his cottage advertising his rabbit hutches for sale.

Sonny's rabbit hutches were, to say the least, appalling botch-ups, and carelessly made. They were not much more than a few pieces of wood with wire strung across them. No countryman would have bought one, but Sonny set out to make a living from the newcomers.

I remember being at his cottage with my sister Pamela one day, when a rather snooty London couple turned up at Sonny's front door, having seen the sign. They said they'd moved to Norfolk and wanted to buy a hutch for their daughter's rabbit.

Sonny tried to sell them a poorly-made hutch that had several holes in the floor. In fact, they were large enough for a fat pet rabbit to fall through.

"I must say we don't think it's very well made," said the husband, pointing to the botch-up of holes at the bottom of the hutch.

"Nar, I build 'em like that. You gotta let the shit and piss get out somewhere, haven't you," he explained to the unconvinced customer.

Hard times in Norfolk...

In the 19th century, when times were hard and people in the countryside often went hungry, a harsh view was taken by landlord and tenant farmer of poaching, especially those who employed a game-keeper and who ran winter shoots for the amusement of the privileged classes.

Penalties were harsh for those working men who were caught trespassing taking game and rabbits from the land of their social superiors. There was little compassion from the rich for those at the bottom of the social scale and Norfolk was no exception to that.

Even up to the start of the First World War, poachers who got caught were fined a week's wages and there were many cases in and around the village. Somehow Charlie managed to evade the law. By the 1950s poaching cases were rare at the local magistrates' courts in Norfolk and Charlie never seemed to show any anxiety when we were afoot at night under a full moon.

Tenant farmers who let a bit of shooting could not afford a game-keeper and wild game was reasonably abundant in south Norfolk – one of the last areas of the county where the hedges were stripped out into prairie.

Charlie, however, perhaps aware of the fate of other members his own family before the magistrates, and of times gone by when he was a younger man, took care to reveal to no one that he owned a shot-gun.

"Never be seen carrying a gun bor," he would warn me. It was advice I followed after his death when I poached for game around the district in the late 1950s and early 1960s.

When he needed to carry the rusty old 12-bore about in daylight he would break it down to its three components and conceal the ancient firearm beneath his thick coat. I think he must have had a furtive arrangement with the village constable to supply him with a few pheasants, hare and rabbits - because the policeman never came knocking at our door.

I don't know whether Charlie had a shot-gun licence or not, but it was possible to buy one from the village Post Office for ten shillings and his step-daughter Auntie Karfie worked behind the counter.

Thinking back I can't remember ever seeing a licence, or his ever making mention of one.

Ten shillings, the cost of a licence, was a lot of money in those days.

Catching game...

There were many methods of taking the game and Charlie taught me all of them by the time I was eight years old. After he died, and I was in my teens, I put his teaching to good use effortlessly and became a successful poacher myself in Norfolk, particularly in catching pheasants with snares or gin-traps, or going out at on moonlit nights and quietly getting under trees in the wood with a shotgun.

There are countless memories of creeping along in the dark and getting to a tree we knew held roosting birds. We'd see the silhouette of a bird on a branch in the light of stars and the moon. Fafa would take aim, a Woodbine as ever perched on his lower lip, and fire the gun from close range to the head of the unsuspecting bird.

Ten yards did the job nicely and we'd prefer to be at least half a mile from the nearest farmhouse. The strange thing was that even though the bird could often hear, or even see us, it would choose to remain in the tree for protection….or so it thought.

Using a snare, we'd dig a hole about three inches deep and two inches in diameter. We'd spread corn around it so that some grains would drop in the hole. We'd then set the snare about an inch down the hole.

The pheasant would poke his head down to get to the corn at the bottom and the feathers would catch in the snare on the way out. It would be trapped by the neck.

The gin trap, which is illegal now, would be set by placing wheat and peas in a sticky bitumen mixture in the middle of the jaw plate. The pheasants would have to peck hard to get at the wheat and peas, setting off the trap. The jaws would slam shut, breaking the bird's neck. It was a highly effective and painless way of killing a bird but deemed by those who thought they knew better than us to be cruel.

"Sod 'em." We thought it was all about securing dinner.

These were wild pheasants, so they were considerably more wary than the semi-domesticated birds of the 21st century. The Shotesham Estate, two miles away from Saxlingham Nethergate, was the only one rearing birds for organised shoots. Many would wander off in the direction of Saxlingham Nethergate . We were grateful they did.

There was at least one gamekeeper at Shotesham and so we'd give the estate a wide berth. There was no point in taking a risk, when a good number of the reared pheasants had migrated conveniently onto the land worked by the tenant farmers, who were usually prepared to turn a blind eye to Charlie's poaching. It left us plenty of ground to choose where to lay our traps and stalk our prey.

Charlie would set up to 50 rabbit snares and gin-traps within a mile and a half of the village, in the big hedges and ditches which ringed most of the fields, and he would remember exactly where each one had been set.

We'd come home each time with a stick full of rabbits across our shoulders – me from the age of four years sometimes laden with the dead creatures. I think Fafa found it amusing I wanted to go with him and learn how to poach, but somehow he seemed to treat me as a grown-up, which I appreciated.

In those days no one was about at night, or early in the morning. Leisure walking, countryside walkers, caravans and campers from the city were something still in the future and the poacher could roam at will without being disturbed.

Although he was a poacher, Fafa always used to say to me that we should never shoot game birds until the leaves were off the trees. We could carry on shooting through the winter, until the buds reappeared on the trees and in the hedges. Then we should stop. That's how he classified the breeding season. We could shoot rabbits and pigeons throughout the year, he said.

He also kept decoys for pigeon shooting on spring-drilled corn and I've still got four at home that Charlie used. We'd watch during the week where the pigeons were going down to feed, build a hide in the hedge, and place the decoy to entice the birds into the killing area. Sometimes a large flock would come down and present good targets at no more than 30 yards, perhaps providing Charlie with three or four birds from one shot. It was glorious to be out in the hide at dawn, waiting for the pigeons to come in.

When we were in Norfolk on our summer holidays, towards the end of his life, when he could no longer be so active, Fafa would sometimes give me a box of 25 cartridges. He'd let me use his secret gun in the Ash tree without him being there. Mind you, he expected to see the results of my shooting in his larder, because for a farm labourer cartridges were expensive.

If I used 10, he wanted to see 10 birds or rabbits. I did not dare miss my target because I was desperate not to disappoint him. I'd come home and find him at the cottage.

"How many you got, bor?" he would ask.

"I shot one cartridge Fafa."

"What did you get?"

"I missed it."

"Bloody missed it?" he'd shout, in mock irritation.

Other things we country boys did were bird-nesting during the season and fishing on the River Tas. This meandered across the common a mile or so from the village. There was one deep hole there called the 'Blunderbus', which people would fish in the autumn and winter for roach and pike. An occasional wild trout was caught.

I had a rod made out of an army khaki tank aerial, which looked splendid. My mother's cousin 'Twag' put some eyes on the tube and tied a cheap little reel onto the bottom. He also made me a few hooks but I never caught anything because they were too big.

In the summer months we children from the local villages would swim in the River Tas. Looking back, I don't think it was very clean but we never caught any infection from swimming.

'Twag' introduced me to sea fishing. He'd take me with him every October to Lowestoft to fish for cod off the pier. We'd catch the bus from Saxlingham to Norwich and then we'd catch the train from Norwich to Lowestoft.

He reckoned the cod were due to start shoaling inshore at that time of year and I remember sitting there shivering, sometimes catching the odd small whiting, which smelled of cucumber.

I think the real reason 'Twag' went to all the trouble to go to Lowestoft was not the possibility of catching cod, but the certainty of eating pie and chips.

"Hey Danny, go get some pie and chips for us," he'd say, handing over half a crown and I'd come back with a feast. We might fetch a bagful from the chip shop two or three times in a day. It was a real treat, because we could not get anything like that in the village. Sometimes, on the way back on the train we'd stop off at Acle on the Broads for a couple of hours bream fishing.

They are illegal now, but in those days we all had birds' egg collections in Saxlingham Nethergate (and later in Stratford) and mine was a source of pride and joy, although it was sometimes hard for me because I did not like heights and was frightened climbing right up trees for the high birds like jackdaws, rooks and crows. Sometimes, though, I made myself do it.

On the way down we'd put the egg in our mouth, even if they were covered in crap. One time I lost my nerve on the descent from one of the magnificent elm trees that used to grow on the Welcombe hills in Stratford and had to be rescued by the fire-brigade---the shame. Stratford fire-brigade was destined to rescue me again, once more from another tricky situation involving childhood antics in Stratford.

The eggs were lovingly set in sawdust or cotton wool and each one was carefully labelled with a name tag to identify the bird. We used to do swaps – like exchanging a blue tit for woodpecker and that sort of thing. Fafa used to help me find the nests. The rarer ones could fetch a good barter – a woodcock's egg for a sherbet dab or a wagon wheel biscuit. The rarest eggs I ever got were whitethroats, or as we called them, "nettle-warblers" because they nested in nettle patches, yellow hammers, nut hatches, tree creepers and gold crests, the latter the country's smallest bird and very difficult to find.

We village boys didn't really have any aspirations of later life and presumed we were going to follow in the footsteps of fathers and grandfathers and work on the land somewhere in Norfolk. We were genuine country lads unaware the world was changing fast around us. What we did aspire to, however, was the village farting championship.

The record at the time was held by Mr Grey, who must have been in his 80s, and who told us he could fart non-stop from the school to the church. This was a distance of about 100 yards.

"You must train if you are going to take my record," he warned us. Somehow it didn't seem at all strange to us young kids that an old man of 80 was telling us how to prolong a fart.

"The natural diet during training is pickled eggs and Guinness. It's easily the best fuel to my knowledge," asserted Mr Grey, who was immensely proud of his achievement, which was carried out while he was in the company of an honest witness to record it, and thus officially verified to the satisfaction of the rest of Saxlingham Nethergate.

Mr Grey also told us boys about the disadvantages of getting older.

"When I was younger I could stand six blackbirds on my cock but now I'm in my 80s I can only accommodate a robin - and that's with it standing on one leg," he said ruefully.

My grandmother Nellie...

My grandmother Ellen, known as Nellie, was from a village family called the Poyntz, who presumed they were of Dutch descent. A family legend held that centuries before, when the Poyntz came to East Anglia, they had been connected to the Dutch Royal Family. A distant relative Georgina Poyntz daughter of William Poyntz married the 4th. Earl Spencer and they had a son John, the 5th Earl Spencer who served in the Royal household, --- that's about as royal as it gets.

There was nothing aristocratic about Nellie. She was a typical farm labourer's wife, with a pinafore and bun, stout of stature, who stopped at home to do the washing in an old copper and cooking on a wood-fuel oven.

She spoke, like Charlie, with a broad Norfolk accent which outsiders would find hard to understand. Nellie was the ultimate mother figure and loved her large brood of seven grandchildren. Nellie had been married twice. Her first husband, a member of the Riches family, was killed in the First World War in Mesopotamia (Iraq).

This meant I had a step-aunty called Kathleen - or Karfy as we called her - and she turned out to be a saint in my childhood, looking after me in the troubled times to come in later years in

Stratford-upon-Avon. Karfy was more of a mother to me than my real mum Mabel and I don't know how I would have coped with the misery of those otherwise loveless years in Stratford without her. Everyone thought the world of Karfy.

She only ever had one boyfriend. Archie was killed in the Second World War and so she devoted her life to looking after other members of the family who needed her, some of whom were our neighbours in the row of terraced cottages. These included my great uncles, who had never married and needed caring for.

Nellie's food was simple and delicious. She would bake bread, cakes, biscuits, meat pies and stews and we'd get two hearty meals a day, wanting for nothing. The aroma of my grandmother's cooking always pervaded the cottage as soon as we walked in.

On Sundays we would have a big joint of roast beef with large swathes of Yorkshire pudding and thick gravy accompanied by vegetables from the allotment. Paradoxically, beef in those days was cheaper than chicken.

We kept hens so we were never short of fowl for the table. When a bird had finished her egg-laying cycle she would be boiled in Nellie's large saucepan. Then she'd be roasted on the range with delicious stuffing that combined wonderfully with the thick gravy. Everything then seemed to have a stronger flavour than today's supermarket food.

There were so many wild pheasant in those days that if we came across a nest with a clutch of 15 or 20 eggs in it we'd break one to check they were not addled, and if they weren't we'd take them back home. Nellie would make an egg custard out of them. We'd do the same with moorhens' eggs.

Our neighbours were really part of the extended family, as we were related to three of the four. They were always in our house, sometimes for meals. There were Goody and Ted Poyntz, and on the other side of us three bachelor Poyntz brothers of my grandmother.

They were called Albert, known as 'Pinky', Cecil, and Isaac, nicknamed 'Ikey.' The latter was a very odd character with a shock of white hair who dressed in clothes from Victorian times. Isaac never spoke. Throughout my childhood he remained completely mute and is said to have never spoken again after his mother told him, when he was a boy, to shut his mouth up.

He'd sit in his old arm chair engaging people with his eyes only. I don't think he ever worked, but his family looked after him. The Clarke family, who were not relations, had the fourth cottage in the terrace.

In the summer we'd use the long table at the back of the house and sit round it, laughing and joking. Those hot and dry Sunday afternoons under a blue cloudless sky were like something out of a scene from the popular TV series *The Darling Buds of May*.

Sometimes we'd crack open crabs bought from Cromer, when the grown-ups had been able to borrow one of the cars in the village to go and fetch them. The kids and the women would drink pop and the men would quaff jugs of local cider. Nellie would serve freshly-baked bread and cakes hot from the oven with home-made farm butter, which had such a pungent flavour that you could still taste it in your mouth an hour later

The cottage was two up and two down. In the kitchen sitting/dining room, where we spent most of our time, there was a large enamel sink which we would fill from the well at the back of the house. Buckets of this pure well water were kept in the larder to keep them cool and they were placed over the range when we wanted hot water for a bath, or when Nellie did the washing on a Monday.

Our home was one of four terraces in a row near the centre of the village and had the kitchen sitting-room and a front best-room for Sundays and special occasions. I was born in that front room and my grandparents both died in the same room.

There was no bathroom, running water or flush toilet downstairs and up the narrow stairs there were just two bedrooms. My brother and I slept in one room with Nellie and Auntie Karfy. Fafa had his own room, due to the odd hours he kept because of his poaching. After he died I inherited his room.

For much of my childhood, until the late 1950s when an electric oven was installed, Nellie cooked on the wood fuel range and our lighting came from paraffin oil lamps. It all seemed natural. Following electrification, it was some years before any of the village people saved up enough money to buy one of the small nine-inch black and white televisions that could be seen in shop windows in Norwich.

Goody and Ted Poyntz were the first of our neighbours to buy one. I'll never forget half the village turning up to look through their window in wonder, as they watched a cowboy western on the first night after the tiny TV set was delivered.

"Them wagon-wheels look like they goin' backards," said one old Poyntz uncle, laughing as he watched the horse-drawn wagons fleeing a band of screaming Indian warriors. This was something new and really exciting for the villagers.

The four cottages are still there, and although they've been modernised and slightly extended they are more or less as they were. My sister Pamela owned Nellie's cottage at one time, but sold it. She's regretted doing that ever since.

Nellie worked part time at the Manor for Mrs Campbell Steward, the squire's wife, and occasionally cleaned houses up Church Hill, the moneyed end of Saxlingham Nethergate, where the rural middle-classes, like lawyers, doctors and owners of businesses in Norwich lived.

She was also the person in the village who laid out the dead, to get them ready and cleaned up for the undertaker and funeral. There were several hundred people living in and around Saxlingham Nethergate, so Nellie was kept quite busy.

Nellie was an ardent churchgoer at St Mary the Virgin Church and helped to decorate it with flowers, corn-dollies and food offerings during the season, especially the harvest festivals.

I was expected to attend church every Sunday. This was a bore for me, especially on a fine day because I wanted to be out in the fields with Fafa. The only vicar I remember was the Reverend Hearn who committed suicide in his car with his dog in 1964, using a hosepipe connected to the exhaust tucked inside the car, while the engine was running.

I asked 'Charlo' English why the vicar had killed himself. He said darkly that I was too young to know. It was certainly a scandal in the village and Ronnie my cousin, who was in the choir, said evasively that he didn't know anything about it either.

Nothing as dramatic as the vicar's suicide had happened in Saxlingham Nethergate since 1944, when the pilot of a bomber was laid out in the doorway of the Cricketer's Arms, after his plane crashed on the edge of the village. There were many RAF and US bomber bases in Norfolk and Suffolk by the end of the War, perhaps more aerodromes than anywhere else.

My first day at work was on the English farm at Christmas 1962 and I milked the entire herd on my own. 'Charlo', the farmer's only son, taught me how to milk. He was at least 20 years older than me and kept me in line when I was helping out on the farm, which he had taken over from his father.

'Charlo' had taught young soldiers to ride during the war in the Army, and in later years had a preference for wearing khaki working clothes or military combat fatigues. He confided to me once in jest when I was a small kid that he was really an escaped German prisoner-of-war hiding in Norfolk from the British Army.

I took it seriously because his blond hair and sun- tanned weather- beaten face made him look German. I went home and decided that night it was my duty to recapture 'Charlo' and hand him over to the village policeman.

I managed to get hold of a bow and arrow and ambushed him in Wash Lane as he was driving the tractor back to the farm. I must have been a reasonable shot because the arrow struck him on the side of the face. He leapt off the tractor, grabbed hold of me and gave me a good thrashing…it was a great shot though.

A new face in the village.

It was something special when Olive arrived and I can remember my first glimpse of this beautiful woman from London, who suddenly came into our tight-knit community.

In 1953 'Charlo' met a delightful East End girl from Hoxton called Olive Gloyn who was highly intelligent, artistic and self-educated. She had previously been the sweetheart of Arnold Wesker, the poet and playwright, before he became famous, when they both lived in London.

He describes her in his autobiography *Arnold Wesker – As Much As I Dare* (Century).

"*Olive Gloyn had a voice that leapt around with dirty, deep-throated, slightly Cockney cadences; a fresh face, high cheekbones, green eyes that laughed in the way only women's eyes can, moving between mockery and a milky lust.*

"*She was youth at the brink, looking out on a world as though anything could happen…..Olive's appeal was a mixture – her eyes glowed with the promise she saw in all things, and I felt she looked upon me as one who might dare what her background rendered her too timid to contemplate. She read a lot, lived in her head and dreams. We were drawn to each other and fell passionately in love.*"

Olive broke Arnold's heart. This happened when she and Arnold left London and went to live with his sister Della and her husband Ralph, who lived on a small-holding nearby at Wacton. Having been evacuated to the Leicestershire countryside during the War, this East End girl had already decided in her mind that she would turn her back on sophisticated urban life, mixing with poets and artists, and marry a farmer instead.

In a letter to me Sir Arnold explained what happened.

"We met in Stoneham's bookshop in the city of London; even in those early days she had expressed a wish to live a country life rather than an urban one. By the time we moved to live with my sister and brother in law in Norfolk I had accepted that fact even though being unhappy with it.

Nevertheless, I reasoned – with illogical and rather feeble chivalry – that if I really loved Olive I would help her find the rural husband she wanted. To which end I suggested we (she and I, not including my sister) should attend local dances pretending we were brother and sister thus leaving her free and available. It was in this guise that Charlie English entered our lives."

At one of the village dances she spotted 'Charlo', a blond and sun-tanned young man, who seemed to be on his own. He was completely bowled over by the scatty and vivacious girl with the London accent, who made it clear she fancied him.

I remember them courting. Charlo owned a little Fiat 500 and I used to go to Norwich Market with them on a Saturday morning with 'Charlo' driving, Olive in the front passenger seat and young Danny crammed into the tiny back seat.

The wedding took place in 1954, but I was considered too young, or more to the point, I owned no smart clothes to go to the service. She was a stunning bride and everyone in Saxlingham Nethergate turned out on their return to the village to see the handsome couple emerge from their car hand in hand for photographs to be taken.

Olive of course remembers her wedding day as she was certainly the centre of all attention. She wrote to me recently: "Why we didn't marry in Saxlingham was because I had no money at all and couldn't stage a "posh" wedding. Dad gave me £50 which he borrowed. My friend's mother made my dress and Freda and Mrs English made some dresses for the little bridesmaids. Mrs Chadwick, landlady of the *Old Barge*, did my 50 guests proud at £1 a head and Charlie whisked me off to Wells in Somerset. Actually, I wanted to go to Cornwall, but never mind. There was no money left for a second week in the four-star hotel, so we finished our honeymoon among the sheep in the Black Mountains."

Olive later told me 'Charlo's' mother, Mrs English, was horrified when she first met her son's fiancé. She reckoned Olive couldn't cook or look after animals, and had no idea of the seasonal farming cycle. It was the worst possible scenario for the English family. She had wanted her only son to marry a Norfolk girl, who had also been brought up on a farm. The city girl from the East End, she thought, was an unsuitable match for 'Charlo', who would soon be taking over the farm.

"You best go back where you come from young lady, village life ain't for you," she told Olive right then and there in no uncertain terms. Olive did not heed her prospective mother-in-law's advice and spent a happy life as a farmer's wife, bringing up her four children and keeping an affectionate and maternal eye on the youngsters of those who worked for 'Charlo' on the farm.

She was always very approachable. At harvest-time Olive and Nellie would bring out what was called 'a bit of bait' for the workers early in the evening, which consisted of a large bottle of cold tea, homemade cake and sandwiches. We'd sit under the shade of a large oak tree, eat our picnic and crack jokes, which were mainly about Suffolk people—did they not like each other?, I thought at the time.

I was among those youngsters who benefited greatly from being mentored by this extraordinary woman. Our cottage was only a five minute walk from the farmhouse and I used to enjoy our talks. Olive seemed to ask me different sorts of questions about schooling and I think this was her way of teaching me to express myself. She is still my close friend and remains a very interesting person.

Now she lives in retirement and widowhood in Saxlingham Nethergate, in a bungalow next to the village hall, built on my grandfather's old allotment. She keeps in contact, always eager to know about my family news and how the world is treating me. I think she makes everyone she knows feel special. I first set eyes upon her 57 years ago, so we share memories of many things.

Olive came to be, and still is, widely loved and admired in the village, closely involved in amateur dramatics and other artistic events; always encouraging others to do challenging things. Arnold Wesker wrote a famous poem in suppressed rage, dated 20th January 1954, about the loss of his beloved Olive to a simple farmer.

Take him, this farmer then,
Over the fields in your arms.
Spin him out on your skin
About the moon in your lap till the pen
In your tongue has worn him thin.

Take him then, this fair-haired man,
Burst your wonderful ways
In the damp ricks of barley corn
And there, lay, and love and plan
The world again where we had shorn

Apart. Take up where we lost touch
And go, go dance with him
This better boy. Soon the Spring
And countryside will crouch
To catch your love and laughing

Cover, comfort and cover
The man alive in you now.
Now you have him
You need not long for the last lover –
He has grown wild and lean
Anyhow, Then with your lips
Rise to him, reach. Open
Your loins and lay, lie
For him, turn him with your finger tips
And chain him to the sky

Hold his hand, go run, go make
New sounds again. Bury
Bad bones and be his wife
Living demands that you break
Your beautiful bodies on life
Have him then, finger his ring
And keep him. Heavens! hide him
Away among blood and bone
And love, laugh, do anything –
But God! Leave me alone.

Sir Arnold explained to me in 2011: "The anger of the 'angry poem' was directed both ways – at Olive, and inwards to myself."

Arnold and Olive became friends again later and she followed his career with both pride and delight. They are still in contact with one another.

Poor old 'Charlo' was never able to conceal his jealousy for Arnold Wesker and probably felt insecure about his wife's continuing, but entirely innocent, association with the (by now) world- famous playwright, who had been her lover.

I remember later in life I came across an autobiography of the playwright in a bookshop while on holiday in Devon. I couldn't wait to tell Olive of my discovery thinking, stupidly, that she didn't know of it and that she was in it.

When I first mentioned it to Olive in the kitchen of the farmhouse she immediately put her fingers to her lips and said: "Shush – don't let Charlie hear what you are saying."

I was slightly confused by her reaction but outside, in the privacy of the front garden, she explained to me her difficult situation.

A picture of the village...

The two neighbouring villages of Saxlingham Nethergate and Saxlingham Thorpe are about seven miles south of Norwich, a mile off the A140 road to Ipswich, where two little valleys join and lead down the River Tas. These once held quite wide tributaries but by the 20th century had been reduced to ditches.

The area may have been first settled in the Neanderthal period, perhaps 50,000 years ago. So our furthest ancestors would have lived among the straight-tusked elephant, bear, rhinoceros, deer and oxen. Eventually, about 12,000 years ago the last Ice Age came to an end.

The climate for what would one day become Norfolk slowly improved until deciduous and temperate plants grew and the modern landscape was created. The rural culture of England, as we know it, evolved over nearly two thousand years from before Roman Times.

Farm rents in Saxlingham Nethergate in the 1950s were reasonably low, as were rates on land and property at that time. There were 12 tenants with farms or small-holdings on the Steward estate and these included the English, Cudden, Emms, Simmons, Stevenson, Youngman, Ward and Moore families.

In the post Second World War period, unlike the 1930s, farming was again profitable as the United Kingdom, ridden with debt, strived to grow as much of its own food as possible and limit the expense of importing meat and grain.

The Stewards at the Manor House kept rents low and this enabled their tenants to continue mixed farming long after the hedges had been ripped out elsewhere in Norfolk and replaced by a prairie landscape for cereal crops.

Time was running out for the tenant farmers, however. One by one, including 'Charlo's' sons, they gave up mixed farming and relinquished their lease. They had no choice but to make way for the larger-scale arable production. These tenant farming families had, for the most part, moved out of the village by the late 1970s.

A survey made by the village school-children in 1963 revealed all 12 tenant farmers still had livestock, mainly dairy cattle. All kept under 20 cattle, except for the English family whose herd by then numbered thirty.

Two farmers kept sheep with about 30 in each flock and most of the farmers kept pigs. Mr Emms had about 100 animals. Soft fruit was widely cultivated, generally looked after by wives, and all farms grew cereals, sugar- beet, beans and peas.

The advent of the family motor car and bus services changed many villages in Norfolk soon after the First World War, but Saxlingham Nethergate had no bus service in the 1950s and remained fossilised in the traditional rural way of life its people had known for more than 100 years. There was, however, a carrier's cart which made possible shopping expeditions to Norwich for the majority, who had no car.

This late reaction to the changes elsewhere in Norfolk in the second half of the 20th century was mainly because Reginald Steward and later his widow Mrs Campbell Steward, as life-tenant of the estate, were determined to preserve the character of the village and were caring and generous benefactors held in high esteem.

As a widow Mrs Steward exercised a benevolent dictatorship making sure that electricity when it arrived ran underground, so no ugly wires and pylons spoiled the look of the countryside.

She was also largely responsible for our War Memorial on the village green in the centre of the village. It was more elaborate than most and had won awards for its design in 1921, unveiled on Armistice Day in November that year.

This was followed by a procession of old soldiers in which Charlie, my grandfather wearing his medals, was photographed marching near the front of the column. The memorial recorded not only the 16 men who lost their life in the Great War, but also the name of every man who had served his country.

Between the world wars Mrs Steward also built the village hall and supported good causes such as the Red Cross, the Guides and other social services including the nursing service. She was also a benefactor of St Mary the Virgin Church, which has the oldest stained-glass windows in the county.

The village hall in my day had a youth club, bingo and hosted a travelling cinema which was packed out on Saturday nights, until the arrival of television meant most people preferred to stay at home. When Mrs Steward died in 1973, Saxlingham Nethergate was still a unique corner of the county which continued to resemble the Edwardian era with its one street, with a wood and a small stream on one side, and a slight slope leading up to the church, which in Norfolk would pass for a hill.

Before my time, earlier in the century, there had been two butchers, a baker, a dairy, two general stores, a blacksmith, a cobbler, a post office and two small sweet shops – plus at least seven pubs. Artisans living in the village worked for a range of small companies or on their own behalf.

By 1953, when Olive came to live in the village, skilled men like carpenters, plasterers, builders and electricians were employed by the Weedon family who were also the undertakers.

There were only two shops, the post office, bakery and the blacksmith forge. The locals had to make do with just five pubs; *The Victoria, The Queen Adelaide, The Cricketers Arms, the Prince of Wales* and *the Bowling Green Inn*, serving a population of a few hundred people – significantly before the arrival of television.

They were all rural pubs, but each landlord managed to make a living. As children we would congregate outside whichever pub our respective father, or grandfather, was drinking in, playing darts and dominoes in the smoky atmosphere on the Victorian settles.

There would be my older brother Cavan, my cousin Ron Riches, the Cudden brothers and Cavan's mate Cally Glanfield; also the Ward brothers Brian and Owen who were excellent boy poachers.

We youngsters stayed outside in the adjoining barn or cart shed, buying our pop and crisps from the off-sales hatch at the back of the bar. If it was winter we would sit in the pitch black. I've no idea what we used to talk about, but I was normally the youngest in the group so did most of the listening.

Inside the pub the regulars would have their beer – frothy glass mugs of Stewart and Pattersons or Bullards - warmed up on a saucepan on the fire and they'd pay perhaps a shilling for a pint. There was no excessive drinking or drunkenness in Saxlingham Nethergate and fights were unknown in the 1950s. People could not afford to binge-drink in those days. Fafa liked his Friday or Saturday night pints of bitter, but on the next morning would be up and about well before dawn to go poaching, so he did not want to be lumbered with a hangover.

One of the two remaining shops was a relic of the general store of Edwardian times, which seemed to sell whatever you might need except for food. An old chap called Pin Yellop, who was less than five feet in height with a withered leg, ran the emporium.

He sold a vast range of stock from wire netting to Wellington boots, to spades and forks, rat traps, Tilly lamps, cartridges, outdoor clothing and boots to name just a few things. I enjoyed going to see 'Pin', because I was curious about what was in there.

Poor old Pin had a severe limp and found it difficult to walk. He was an amiable chap but didn't trust a soul, so his cabinets were covered in wire. It meant no one could open the drawers unless he was there. I don't know why he thought we were going to pinch anything, considering we didn't lock our own doors in those days. The smell of that shop has stayed with me to this day. It was a wonderful place.

The general store was just the other side of the War Memorial and was called Brightons. It sold fresh fruit and vegetables, a large range of tinned food, confectionery, soft drinks and cordials, paraffin and kitchen goods. We could also order meat from the next village, where there was a butcher. There was no frozen food in those days.

My favourite place, however, was Funnel the baker. We'd knock on the hatch door at the side of the bakery and enjoy the strong fragrance of bread baking in the ovens. My own partiality was for Mr Funnel's doughnuts, which I still miss.

Up to this point I've mostly described the people in my childhood whom I loved and who seemed to love me. Now it's time to introduce the two people who intentionally or unintentionally brought me grief, dismay and ongoing unhappiness during my early years through either neglect or disinterest. These two people were my father and mother, Jack and Mabel (Mary) Keaney.

Chapter Two
A DYSFUNCTIONAL FAMILY

My mother Mabel, of course, was Norfolk born and bred. She was in her early 20s when she met my father, a tall dark-haired Irish navvy with a limp from Glenfarne, County Leitrim, on an RAF base sometime in 1941. She was working in the NAAFI and Jack, who was in his 30s, was over here, like thousands of other Irishmen, building aerodromes in East Anglia.

Mabel was Charlie and Nellie's only child, although she had an older step-sister and step-brother. In her youth she was the village beauty, with long black hair, dark brown eyes and a slim figure. She soon fell in love with Jack, who appeared to be educated and from a good family and with an outgoing nature that made him popular with others.

They married in a catholic church in Norwich and hosted the reception in the village hall, and then soon afterwards Jack took her off with him, working all over the country on War Ministry contracts.

Mabel returned to Saxlingham Nethergate after giving birth to my brother, Cavan, and left her baby after a few months with Charlie and Nellie, before rejoining Jack somewhere in the United Kingdom.

The same thing happened with Kathleen and with Pamela, born while Jack and Mabel were working in Southampton. The birth of both girls were a surprise to Charlie and Nellie because my parents never bothered to write to them and on each occasion Mabel turned up at the cottage in the village for them to look after.

I should imagine my grandparents were delighted at the unexpected opportunity, provided by the war, of having a family of young children to care for all over again. I came along in 1947 after the war and was followed by three younger sisters Ann, Maureen and Eileen; the two youngest Maureen and Eileen were born in Stratford-upon-Avon.

Cavan and I were never to share the loving childhood experiences of our female siblings, although for my brother the sense of parental neglect was ameliorated because he spent almost his entire childhood and adolescence in Norfolk, being cared for affectionately by Charlie, Nellie and later Auntie Karfy. I think he was luckier than me.

"Come on you little shit or you'll get left behind," said the big Irishman who was still a virtual stranger to me, but whom I knew to be my father. We were about to undertake a long journey and I had been delaying our departure by hiding under the bed. I didn't want to leave Fafa and Nellie.

There was no kindness in his voice. This man was no Fafa. There was barely suppressed irritation in the attitude of the man who was my father and things never got better between us. As for my mother, I don't think Mabel ever took me in her arms for a hug or a cuddle in my entire childhood, and most of the time she was cold and distant towards me.

It was 1952. I was five years old and just about able to understand that I was leaving Norfolk to live somewhere called

Stratford-upon-Avon in the Midlands. In fact, Jack had managed to get a good job as works foreman with a company called Lumley Saville. He would no longer be just a navvy and he'd decided it was time for us all to settle down in one home.

I think Charlie and Nellie must have been alarmed at what was happening. Mabel already had five children and being an only and much adored child she had been spoiled as a youngster. She had grown up to be rather a selfish person, with a quick temper, who expected to get her own way.

As she became a woman it was clear to everyone she lacked the maternal instincts of her step-sister Karfy and her mother Nellie. At the start of the war, as a very young woman, she had worked at a munitions factory just outside Norwich. Auntie Karfy used to cycle with her to Norwich, return to the village, and then cycle in again at the end of Mabel's shift before escorting her back again. They wouldn't let her go on her own. She was their princess and had to be closely protected and want for nothing.

There's no doubt that during the War, when Jack was travelling all over the country Mabel enjoyed the excitement of being her new husband's constant drinking and social companion, without the irritating constraint of children. She was free to be with him whenever she pleased.

When all this ended after the War, she found herself burdened with the responsibilities of keeping home and motherhood and she resented it. That is the only way I can make any sense of her disinterest in me, which lasted until the end of her life. I could never understand why she treated her girls so much better than me. Having said that about

Mabel's disinterest in me, I must admit she became a brilliant grandmother later in life.

I was about to begin a childhood that in many ways was a dichotomy. I was to spend years being shunted backwards and forwards, sometimes because I would hide and miss the car back to Stratford. During these years I attended six schools.

When I was in Norfolk I lived a blissful and loving existence. My Stratford years, on the other hand, were overshadowed by living in a dysfunctional family whose head liked the occasional drink. I found myself growing up in a brutalised working class community, where violence was the norm, and childhood was a challenging proposition for both me and my peer group.

Ironically, the world saw Stratford-upon-Avon as a picture postcard mediaeval town of half-timbered buildings and a theatre overlooking the River Avon, dedicated to the work of William Shakespeare. But here was a parallel universe. Stratford had another face, a brutal and sneering face, which the great Bard himself may have been familiar with in his own youth 400 years before.

It was not the picture postcard place people assumed it to be, but a rather mean working class market town with strict class demarcations. It had been a violent melting pot during the Second World War with British, American and Canadian servicemen all stationed nearby and rubbing shoulders with thousands of civilian factory workers, who had been shipped into the town to do war work. At times the local police had to work hard to stay in control, especially at weekends.

My first glimpse of Stratford...

I can remember leaving Fafa's cottage in the village as if it was yesterday. I was crying and it made it worse to see them waving from the side of the road as the heavy vehicle, with Lumley Plant painted on the side, clanked off down the lane carrying its cargo of children and furniture.

Eventually, I settled down to a long sleep, interrupted only by cheese and chicken sandwiches and a flask of tea, provided by Nellie. My three sisters Kathleen, Pamela, and even baby Ann, seemed to regard the expedition into the unknown with more excitement than I did. I felt totally uprooted and out of my comfort zone.

At this age I had never experienced or even seen a town. I had never even been taken to see Norwich. So our eventual arrival in Stratford-upon-Avon was deeply disturbing to me. There were many more people than I had ever seen before, and traffic which drove in long lines nose to tail and seemed to be part of some procession. Then there were the exhaust fumes, squat ugly houses, factories and red brick office blocks.

It was my first experience of the urban nightmare and already I longed for the birdsong, fields, the horse, cow and pig shit and other smells of the rural Norfolk countryside - and the reassuring smallness of the cottage in Saxlingham Nethergate.

"Over there girls, that's where I go to work!" said the tall man with spectacles to his girls Kathleen and Pamela as we passed the half-built headquarters of Lumley Saville on the Birmingham Road, Stratford. We were nearly there after many hours of driving.

I did not notice much about any of the office buildings along the Birmingham Road except that they were ugly and square and my attention became fixed upon what seemed to be an enormous hole in the ground to the rear of them. This was filled with monstrous iron and steel creations out of some horror story. I stared at it with my thumb in my mouth.

We were told by Jack that these were left over from the war and had been used to fight the Germans. Later, I discovered they were what were called tanks, unwanted Army vehicles, artillery pieces and parts of locomotives, buses and railway carriages. Some were piled up in the air at grotesque angles as if they were the end result of some holocaust.

This horrendous eyesore which dominated the main entrance to Stratford from Birmingham was later to become a favourite and forbidden playground – it's now the Maybird Retail Park - for me and my pals, but then its ugliness and grim and brutal magnitude of scale filled me with a sense of foreboding.

"Where were all the woods and meadows?" I wondered.

The lorry approached the end of its journey and parked outside 18 Maple Grove, off Justin's Avenue. It was a brand new red brick semi-detached council house with a hall, kitchen and front and back room downstairs - and three bedrooms and a bathroom upstairs. It was the first time we children had ever seen a proper upstairs bathroom with running water and a flushing toilet. I was really rather intrigued by a flushing toilet and for the first few days used to wave goodbye to my turd as I pulled the chain.

The kitchen had a sink with hot and cold water and storage units, plus a gas cooker. My mother had brought with her a copper for the washing and an old-fashioned mangle. There was a shed attached to the house, a coal-bunker and an outside toilet. The garden was still field turf and remained uncultivated for several years because Jack was no gardener.

Later, a man came and laid some slabs on the heavy clay soil. I remember as we arrived on the lorry that some men, at the other houses, were pushing mowers laboriously, trying to create lawns. The nearest we ever came to having a family garden was an old steel swing that a neighbour gave us in the first year.

It seemed to me, after living in rural Norfolk, in a rather primitive and cluttered family country cottage, that our new home was bare and unfriendly. It smelled of new paint and also of the lino that covered the wooden board flooring.

Jack and Mabel had saved up to buy some furniture and also received hand-me-downs from generous members of the family in Norfolk. Gradually, these were put in place to make a home of our new house. There was to be no television until Coronation Day in 1953 when we bought a nine inch screen Fergusson TV.

On our first night I slept in the same room as Pamela, while Kathy and Ann were in another – later to share a room with my Aunt Karfy – and Jack and Mabel were in the main bedroom. It might have seemed we were a new happy family in the making, but somehow things did not turn out to be like that.

Having said this about our new surroundings, it was I who really disliked Stratford, Justin's Avenue and Maple Grove - rather than my siblings, who were filled with a sense of adventure and upon whom Mabel devoted all her limited affection.

Some people had arrived on the estate before us, but really it was like a new colony or settlement in a strange land. Most incomers were not local but from various parts of the country, brought in to work in the many local factories that needed labour, and most of the new arrivals were well schooled in the art of survival.

At this stage, of course, I was too young to understand about the social background of our neighbours and how they would gel as a community. They were nearly all a hardened bunch, who had known previously only an urban way of life in the slums in the 1930s and 1940s. I had known and taken for granted only a tight-knit rural village, where many of the families were related and where people looked out for one another - and above all we were well fed.

I had always understood that Jack was my father, but he seemed to make a point of ignoring me. He left me feeling as though I was an unwanted outsider. That may not have bothered me too much in my infancy. While Fafa spent time with me and was introducing me to his way of life, I did not care a hoot about the attitude of this cold and distant father with an Irish accent.

Now I was away from Norfolk I was in Jack's domain and this intensified my hatred of the new surroundings, even though I was still not much more than a toddler.

My first hiding...

During the first few weeks in Stratford, my mother found me to be an irritation hanging around the house. I think I was shy and unwilling to go out and explore and introduce myself to children of my own age. There were many weeks of summer holiday lying ahead and she felt that being a boy, I should seize the initiative and go out and mingle with the local lads of my peer group. The girls were allowed to stay around the house and help out.

"I've been to see Mrs Brook who lives in one of the houses at the back of ours in Hodgson Road and she has a son of about your age called Colin. She says you can go and play with him today. So I don't want you in the house hanging around under my feet – go find Colin and meet some of his pals."

I duly obeyed and walked round to Hodgson Road hoping to find a new friend. I walked to outside his house – which looked out across the green - and was about to knock on the front door when a dark-haired boy suddenly appeared from around the corner and shot me at close range with his catapult. The stone hit me hard on my knee. He found this amusing and then punched me in the face.

"Piss off," he shouted.

I started to cry so he hit me again, doubtless seeing it as an opportunity to enjoy some aggravation against a weaker boy and also, perhaps, to demonstrate his fighting skills to other children on the green over the road.

Colin turned out to be a year older than me, much bigger at that time, and I wasn't going to argue with him. I suppose he considered I was an invader on his territory. He became a close friend when we were much older.

It was not a promising start to life in Stratford and a taste of what was to come. There was no sympathy from Mabel over this violent incident; in fact I didn't even bother to tell her. She was not going to have me messing about in the house for the summer and so I had no choice but to go out and confront my predicament.

Later in life, I always thought it was odd that Mabel should have seven children but usually remained cold in her manner towards us although it has to be said my sisters dispute this. At that time I must have thought it was normal to have indifferent or uncaring parents and it was only by going to visit homes where there was love that I realised the Keaneys were a dysfunctional family.

The world of children around Justin's Avenue was centred on the green, around which many of the houses were built, and less than five minutes walk from the Keaney home. It was known as the "Arab Camp". I have no idea why but local amateur military historian Derrick Smart tells me that while the Clopton Estate was under construction German prisoners-of-war lunched in a large marquee on the Hodgson Road green while they were digging out the drainage system. When they had had lunch all the local children used to sit with them – many a child's birthday gift was a wooden toy made by the prisoners to a very high standard.

A later generation of kids played football and cricket there, made fires, shared secrets and had their endless gang fights. It was a kingdom inhabited by children and adolescents, with a strict pecking order, based on a code of violence.

It was a place where I was on the wrong end of countless beatings and soon came to the conclusion that the only way to protect myself was in being part of a gang. I was by nature a mild-mannered little chap and fighting did not come naturally to me at first. Even my two bigger sisters used to bully me. Big sister Kathleen was a great scrapper and my father used to say that if her eyes didn't cut so easily she would have made a good boxer. This was soon to change and might possibly be what lay at the back of Jack's mind, if he thought about me at all. Perhaps he told Mabel I needed toughening up.

Our gang...

I made friends gradually with some of the boys who were my contemporaries. These included Brian Harrison. He was from a large family of four children and being a Roman Catholic was at St Gregory' Primary School in Henley Street which I attended eventually in my second year in Stratford.

The gang included Mick and Jim McLoughlin, Robert Sharlot, Roy Rogers,(Roy's Dad must have been keen on cowboy comics) Colin Brook, Mervyn Daffin, Spider Tomacek, David and Terry Smith. The Smiths were enemies at first but gradually we made friends with them. Our gang was by no means the toughest on the green because we were barely of school age and so we knew we could expect to get beaten up every day of the week.

Roger 'Spider' Tomacek, a year older than me, had perfected the most lethal head butt. I kept out of his way in any argument but caught his head and right hooks a couple of times. They were both really well executed.

'Fluff' Jones became a member of our gang when he was old enough – he was a year younger than me - and it soon became clear he was a good fighter and enjoyed scrapping. It was a large family, the boys could handle themselves, and they looked out for one another. Jonah was the oldest, who was also a rough nut, then came Peter who was more sensible than the others, (Peter later in life joined the Territorial army in Stratford like many others in the Arab camp simply to get his hands on a sturdy pair of boots to wear when gardening) 'Fluff', and then Barry and David. They could all dish it out and people were very wary of them by the end of the 1950s, especially Fluff.

The Jones had arrived about the same time in Stratford as the Keaneys, also on the back of a Lumley Saville's lorry, because Ted Jones, who was a very good father to his boys, also worked for the company. I was warned about Fluff being a hard nut by one of my pals and to be careful when I first met him.

"He's really ugly so you can't mistake him," I was told by another kid. He turned out not to be quite as ugly as I expected - but wore national health glasses which did not improve his appearance. I found out that his cousin, who was still living in London, had got the part to play the first Milky Bar Kid in the early TV adverts – but he was better looking than Fluff. All the free boxes of Milky bars promised by Fluff never materialised.

The Harris family in Justin's Avenue had two older boys we knew well called Terry and the older brother Mousey, who could also handle themselves and were not scared of the Jones family. One day they pinched Fluff's pet rabbit. He found it had gone when he went to look for it in the hutch in the back garden. When he got back from work, an indignant Ted went round to the council house where the Harris family lived, to get the rabbit back for Fluff.

"Would you like it with the crust on or off?" asked Mrs Harris. They had cooked it for tea. I'm sure Fluff exacted his revenge but I can't remember how.

Every morning you woke up you knew you were going to get it from someone either on the green, somewhere in the Welcombe Hills, Park or Clopton Road, which was our stomping ground.

If you went out alone it was likely you would be confronted by a gang of slightly older kids. They would not bother to talk to you - they would just start punching or slapping you.

You'd try and scarper but they'd surround you so you couldn't get away. If you tried to fight back it would be even worse for you. They'd really go to town on you. It didn't matter if they knew you or not; gratuitous violence was part of the culture. I seemed to wear a permanent black eye and swollen lip but it didn't seem to bother my mother.

"Just fight back, don't let them bully you," she used to say.

One of the gangs a bit further up the food chain than us enjoyed slapping us about whenever they found us. This motley crew comprised of the legendary Archie Davis, Nigel Davis, Jonah, Fluff's older brother, and Hadyn Powell. Even my mother had heard that "He's very good with his hands is Hadyn," which meant his fists of course.

Sometimes it was possible to get help from someone older when the chips were down, but not often. The day came when I had a great opportunity to hammer Hadyn by way of help from the big, strong and sensible John Durnian who also lived in the Justin's Avenue area and was about the same age as the Powell gang.

Hadyn was slapping and punching me and my brother Cavan, who at the time was in Stratford on a break from Norfolk. He was giving us both a lot of 'gyp' on the green and we expected to get a serious hammering. We were at his mercy and onlookers were indifferent to our fate.

Suddenly, Cavan made a break for it, leaving me to suffer my fate at the hands of the menacing Hadyn.

"Hang on Danny for a few minutes, I'll go and get help," he shouted as he 'scarpered' like a young gazelle in the direction of home.

I thought I was done for and abandoned by my older brother. I sensed that what was about to come from Hadyn would at least be a black eye, bloodied nose, and bruises from a good kicking, if I went to ground.

My older brother had not forsaken me. Somehow, he found a saviour in the form of John Durnian. For a reason unknown to us, John decided to help. He rushed over and grabbed Hadyn, throwing him to the ground, where he cowered, waiting for a good kicking. Now the boot was on the other foot. John pinned Hadyn down and waited for me to exact my revenge.

"A punch in the mouth would be just fine," said John looking me square in the face.

I chickened out.

"I forgive him," I said with a look of shame upon my face. What a wimp!

Thank God it was the sensible John Durnian who heard me say that and not some other kids, or I'd never have lived it down. This shy and mild-mannered child, this wimp, could not help but change in such a violent world. And change I did gradually.

The parallel universe...

At the same time that I was being shuttled under protest from Norfolk to Stratford, in my mind from paradise to a violent hell, another young man, who was older than me and an undergraduate at Cambridge, was making an annual journey from his home in Suffolk to the Bard's town, to watch performances at the Memorial Theatre often inspired by the actor/director Anthony Quayle.

His name was Peter Hall and he would cycle all the way from East Anglia, camp alongside the river, and then go to every show for a week at the Memorial Theatre during the summer festival, which sometimes featured big box office names from the world of film.

He realised at that time that he wanted to be a director of theatre and dedicated his life to achieving that ambition, living of course in a privileged parallel universe compared to me and my chums in working class Justin's Avenue.

By the Stratford season of 1958 – and also 1959 – Peter Hall had achieved his ambition and let loose Laurence Olivier (*Coriolanus*), Charles Laughton (*A Midsummer Night's Dream*) and Paul Robeson (*Othello*) and later Edith Evans in productions at the theatre.

There was a rumour going round town that Robeson was turned away from one of the town's top hotels because he was a black man. He ended up lodging with fellow actor Andrew Faulds. On reflection, that really didn't say much for the narrow-mindedness of the land and house-owning class in Stratford, because Robeson, by then, was an established world figure. The fact is a lot of well-to-do Stratford people in the post war period were ignorant of the world outside their town.

A few years later, the Royal Shakespeare Company was founded and among the actors who hit town was Peter O'Toole, the hell-raising, roaring, Irish boy from the North of England. *The Dirty*

Duck enjoyed its second golden era for boozing in the early 60s, shortly before O'Toole embarked on his most famous feature film *Lawrence of Arabia*.

David Lean, who was to produce the film, came to Stratford to see Peter O'Toole play Petruchio, the male romantic lead in *The Taming of the Shrew* and realised he had found his leading man for the film. He persuaded him to abandon Stratford, break his contract with the newly-formed Royal Shakespeare Company, and become a film star.

Peter was the sort of chap who would have fitted in perfectly in Justin's Avenue. He was the loud and extrovert son of a bookmaker, who never backed off a fight with anyone, and enjoyed causing havoc during his stay in Stratford. He would walk around the town uninhibited with his wild hair and beard, and he had to be restrained on more than one occasion, allegedly, by Peter Hall from launching off on one of his heavy drinking bouts, usually at the *Dirty Duck*.

For some years during this post-war era, as the child gangs were growing up on the council estates in Stratford, the town was becoming simultaneously a proving ground for Hollywood; a cycle that has only re-emerged again recently with the success of RSC actors like David Tennant.

Chapter Three

AT SCHOOL IN STRATFORD

Everything must have been marvellous in the life of the young Welsh actor Richard Burton in 1951 and 1952. He made his mark in Stratford as Prince Hal in both *Henry IV* and *Henry V* and then as Ferdinand in *The Tempest*. Burton was celebrated by his contemporaries as a 'roaring boy' in the first boozy post-war era at the Dirty Duck, drinking with Michael Redgrave who was playing Prospero in *The Tempest* and *Richard* in *Richard II*. They were following in the earlier footsteps of Paul Scofield, Donald Sinden and Joss Ackland under the guiding hand of artistic director Anthony Quayle from 1948 to 1956.

Things were less euphoric for the young Danny Keaney in the bleak and depressing scenario of 1952. The only consolation that year was the arrival of my beloved and saintly Auntie Karfy who had been sent to Stratford from Norfolk by an anxious Nellie to come and look after us. She was a wonderful woman and allowed me to bring my troubles to her. I now look back upon her as my real mother.

I believe Charlie and Nellie in Norfolk knew things that we did not know about Mabel. They realised that she was not capable of looking after us properly. I suspect my mother tended to be idle having been spoiled as a child and she seemed happy for others to do her work for her.

I can remember Mabel sitting in the kitchen with her feet up on the chair one morning, reading a book next to the fire, while

Auntie Karfy did all the ironing, washing and cooked meals for us children.

Arrangements had been made for me to start primary school after Christmas in the spring term 1952 at Thomas Jollyffe Church of England School. There was no place for me at St Gregory's Roman Catholic Primary School in Henley Street, although Pamela was sent there before I eventually joined her.

Jack was not, by any means, a devout Christian but wanted us brought up as Roman Catholics. He would sometimes go to Mass and occasionally to Holy Communion. He got pissed with the priests in Stratford more than once. My mother would have had no say in our religion and neither would my grandparents, who were both Anglican.

My first impression was being left at the school by Karfy on my first morning and crying loudly. Pamela was there as well and comforted me – but I hated it. To be fair, Thomas Jollyffe was quite a good school and the members of staff there were generally kind and considerate to their pupils. The playground, however, reflected the underlying sub-culture of violence that I had been exposed to on the estate around Justin's Avenue. Bullying was endemic.

I remember Miss Otter, the head mistress, who was warm and gentle. The teachers tried hard not to be too harsh on their pupils, although corporal punishment (just a short sharp clip if needed) was part of the culture of the school.

I think I soon became a test to the teachers, because I did not show much interest in what was going on in the classroom, was not by nature respectful to authority and tended to prefer to make my own rules, rather than abide by what was laid down in the book.

I do not think I was deliberately naughty or wilful, but as far as schools were concerned I was doomed to be a round peg in a square hole. I did not like being confined to a desk in a classroom, dreamed of the countryside and my recent part in it with Fafa, of farms and what went on in nature's cycle as far as agriculture was concerned. To me, lessons were an irrelevance and I really could not see any point in them.

I was not an aggressive or rebellious child in these very early stages of school life but seemed to find myself cast gradually as the natural rebel. It brought with it trouble from my teachers.

Aunty Karfy the angel...

At home Aunty Karfy tried hard to be the peacemaker between Jack and Mabel, but the rows were constant when he was at home, from the first week that we arrived to live in Warwickshire. There would be a bad one at least once a week. As kids, we never knew what their rows were about. I seem to remember they would be worse when he came home late and his breath smelled of drink. My mother would be shouting the loudest – in her broad Norfolk accent.

"Fuck off back to Norfolk with your sugar beet friends!" he'd shout back.

Then there would be a violent fight in which Mabel might hit him and knock off his glasses – but he would never hit her. He'd just try to push her off, but she had a foul temper and her shouting and screaming must have been audible in the neighbouring houses.

This would happen in front of the kids and we would run upstairs and hide, my sisters crying. Karfy would come up and make sure we were all right. She would try to stop the fighting, but never could. I can remember my mother after one row with her head in the gas oven.

"I'm going to kill myself," she announced hysterically.

This family drama ended up with two sisters trying to pull her out and my brother Cavan with his foot on her arse trying to push her in - and my father in his Irish accent contributing his penny worth.

"For fock's sake, she's old enough to make her own mind up."

I do have an inkling some of the rows were about money, or the lack of it, because even though Jack was a foreman there never seemed to be enough to go round, with so many mouths to feed.

I had come to the conclusion by now that we were not a normal family although I didn't know the meaning of dysfunctional. Jack and Mabel were certainly an unusual couple and quite unpredictable, except perhaps in their consistent disinterest in Cavan and me.

How many houses in the Justin's Avenue area I wonder had a cigarette machine installed in the hall at the bottom of the stair case? We did - and for two shillings we could buy a filter tip packet of 10 Number Six cigarettes. My brother and sisters used to pop in Clyde Higgs milk tokens which fitted perfectly – but judgement day would always come when the representative turned up to unlock the machine to take out the money before refilling it.

Jack would shout: "Who the fock's been putting in those focking milk tokens?"

In the end he'd have to make up the deficit out of his pocket but the machine stayed there for years.

Babies Maureen and Eileen were born soon after we came to Stratford, which meant there were now six children in the house. In fairness, I can accept looking back that it must have been a desperately humdrum life for Mabel after the exciting years of the war. She was surrounded by children and only rarely invited by Jack to go out to the pub with him for a drink.

I stayed at Thomas Jollyffe School for two terms until a place was found for me at St Gregory's Roman Catholic School at the bottom of Henley Street. I spent a year at St Gregory's. Then I was shifted back to Norfolk shortly before I was eight-years-old. The return to Fafa and Nellie came as an extreme relief. Being in Stratford felt to me like being in hell.

St Gregory's was an extremely strict school where the emphasis was less on the 'three R's' and more on instilling religious knowledge and learning the dogma of Roman Catholicism, which I grew to dislike intensely. I particularly hated going to the Roman Catholic Church for Mass on a Tuesday morning, having to do confession and taking Holy Communion from one of the priests.

You weren't supposed to eat before Holy Communion so you took your breakfast to school to eat before lessons started. Mine usually consisted of a hard-boiled egg in my pocket, which I cracked on the desk.

The luckier kids tended to have toasted sandwiches lovingly prepared, no doubt, by their mother. One of these was David

Young, now a well known and respected figure in the town. I asked him once if I could have a piece of his toast, expecting to be rebuffed.

"Of course you can," said David generously, to my great surprise. I should not have been surprised, because that was the sort of boy David was. It is something I have never forgotten, even though more than 50 years has elapsed.

At Confession as we sat inside the confessional box we could see the outline of the priest behind the screen. We were expected make the sign of the cross and then start off with the usual patter.

"Bless me father, for I have sinned."

"And what have you done this week?" the priest would ask.

"Oh, bloody hell here we go again, what the f**** it got to do with you" I'd be thinking.

I might not have done anything wrong at all, but would make things up to satisfy him. It would usually go along the following lines.

"I kicked the cat up the arse this week," I told him. Kicking cats up the arse in the 50s was a regular occurrence. I had not touched the bloody cat, but felt I had to admit to some misdemeanour which was wrong in the eyes of God.

"Go outside and kneel at the altar. Say three Hail Marys and three Our Fathers for penance," the priest would say. I made the sign of the cross in case anyone was looking.

"Get stuffed" I thought to myself. That was me done for another couple of weeks.

I did make some good friends at the Catholic school like Philip O'Brien, Brian Harrison and Christopher Brebner. I remember beating Chris in the final of the 'peeing up the wall' competition in the toilets at St. Gregorys. There were bullies in the playground, but the threat they posed was nothing like as serious as the harsh nature of the lessons where fear reigned.

The memory of some of the teachers at St Gregory's will be etched on my memory for the rest of my life. There was Miss Harman, the headmistress, Miss Richardson, the deputy head, the Irish Miss O'Gara, Miss Scotson, Miss Mulveal and Miss Tippett.

The first two, Harman and Richardson, both in their late thirties, ruled the school strictly - and strongly believed in corporal punishment, which was a daily factor in our classroom education. This would range from a slap in "the chops", the back of the head, the cane on the hands, legs or back of the neck. Looking back, I can only conclude Harman and Richardson were vicious people, who took a wicked delight in punishing children by hurting them.

The two spinsters disliked me and so I was hit or beaten most days of the week for poor work or what they considered to be bad behaviour. One morning I was being beaten on my hands. The first stroke had really hurt me and so to avoid the second I pulled my hand away at the last moment.

Miss Harman, a short rather fat woman with black hair and a bobbed haircut, missed her target and accidentally administered a strong blow to her own leg just above the knee. There was a loud yelp of pain as the cane made contact with her own portly frame and she completely lost control of herself, going berserk with fury.

She spent about a minute setting about me with the cane, hitting me numerous times all over my body. She struck me on the back of the neck, the top of the head, across the legs and arms.

This was in front of the whole class. I must have done something seriously wrong in her eyes and I think, looking back, that I had in a few short months turned from being a mild-mannered inoffensive lad into a classroom rebel with increasing independence of spirit. The violent world I was forced to inhabit was responsible for it. I was never a bully however – and in fact at that time, still only seven years old, I was getting beaten up every day by older children in the playground.

I remember getting a good hiding deservedly from Miss Harman during one spring term when the Swifts were nesting under the eaves of the school. To reach their nest the pairs had to swoop down low and all the kids used to try to catch them. I had the idea of getting hold of a girl's skipping rope and smacking one out of the sky.

I succeeded and was rightly given a caning in front of the school. It was a misdemeanour for which I later felt considerable remorse, as I had a love of animals except, of course, the ones I liked to eat, as Fafa had shown me in Norfolk. I was too ashamed to tell him about it when I returned to Norfolk. Being cruel to animals of any kind was never part of the old man's nature and I was anxious never to disappoint him.

The teachers must have had some faith in me though. On the morning of the Christmas Nativity Play I was delegated the job by Miss Harman of going down to Pargetters the bakers in Bridge Street to buy three small loaves for the Three Wise Men

– who would need it after their journey across the Holy Land. Unfortunately my need was greater than theirs and on the way back to school I was overcome by a sudden attack of ravenous hunger – something to do with the delicious aroma of fresh bread emanating from the paper bag. Before I could do anything to restrain myself – Mable had forgotten to give me any breakfast that day – I had stuffed the wise man's loaf into my mouth and gobbled it down. There was no money in my pocket to buy another.

The wrath of Miss Harman was visited upon me in a beating with her ruler, across my right hand – but I'd already decided it was worth it. That loaf was delicious and I didn't give a bugger about the three wise men anyway. Miss Harman might have done a little forward thinking and used my misdemeanour as portent of further trouble. She had foolishly cast me in the part of the winged angel who walks on stage at the opening of the play and explains to the audience what the Nativity is all about and who is in it.

The school hall was packed with parents in a rare state of anticipation as I walked unconcerned onto the stage in front of them – Jack and Mabel hadn't bothered to come. I stood there ready to deliver my lines but nothing came out of my mouth. I went mute. The audience waited and waited and bottoms began to shift uneasily on seats. I could not remember one word that I was supposed to say and I bloody well wasn't going to ask for divine inspiration. I held the audience for about 30 seconds in silence with strange hisses coming from one of the teachers at the side of the stage. I glanced towards the hissing and at that moment one of my sodding wings fell off and landed with a flop on the stage. With that I was dragged off and given a good shaking. The audience loved it.

Back in paradise...

It was a relief to be sent back to Norfolk for the summer holidays in 1956. In fact, I managed to stay permanently when the time came at the end of August for us to go back to Stratford. I took the law into my own hands and hid outside Saxlingham Nethergate concealed in a ditch, until Jack and Mabel drove away. It meant another year with my beloved Fafa. A week later I pitched up at the village school to enrol.

I was immediately much happier. There was no bullying or oppression from the teachers. In fact, I was left to run free and during this time cultivated my love for being and helping on the farm run by 'Charlo' and Olive, who were having children of their own by now.

I'll never know why I was allowed to stay in Norfolk in 1956 but Auntie Karfy might have been instrumental in the decision not to chase me back, because she was concerned at the number of beatings I was receiving from the teachers at St Gregory's. Of course, it could also have been that Mabel was sick of the sight of me and relieved to have me out of her everyday life. Perhaps Jack allowed it for the sake of a more peaceful life.

This was the year when I started to learn more about poaching and the countryside; the latter is something that has remained my overriding passion in life here in Warwickshire.

I think I might even have been allowed to remain in Saxlingham Nethergate permanently, but Fafa gradually became debilitated with the cancer that was enveloping his lungs - and Cavan and I probably became too much for Nellie to take on permanently, as the old man became more dependent upon her.

So, by early 1957 I was back in Stratford, having been away for a year.

Miss Harman and Miss Richardson were waiting for me, determined to continue to make my life a misery. No doubt they could see that in the year away I had not changed. I was still an unrepentant and poor disciple of the Roman Catholic Church. In their eyes it meant I was a doomed individual and sinner, deserving of no mercy from the Lord.

I clearly remember Miss Harman, wearing her tweed suit and brown brogue shoes, peering at me in a hostile manner on the first morning I was back at her school. Her opening comment in the classroom was to say triumphantly: "That stupid school you've been to down in Norfolk – I see they haven't even taught you to do joined up writing."

At lunchtime we used to go to a hall in Payton Street, where we would have our school dinner. We'd eat at trestle tables with the teachers at a top table on the stage, keeping a watchful eye on their pupils. When we finished our meal we would queue up and empty our plate into a large aluminium bin. We would then sit down at the table and wait to be marched back to the school in Henley Street.

During the second term, the shrill commanding voice of Miss Harman rang out during one lunch time from the top table on the stage.

"Danny Keaney, stand up!"

"Yes Miss Harman."

"Did you just scrape some food into that bin?"

"Yes Miss Harman."

"Go and get it and eat it."

I walked over to the bin in front of the whole school with the plate and fork in my hand and looked inside. It was full of food scraps and I certainly could not remember which of them were mine. She made me pick up the scraps and eat them in front of the children. It remains a puzzle to me why she made me do that since we were allowed to leave a little food when we had no appetite to eat it.

I can only conclude she was a vindictive woman and saw in my discomfort and distress an opportunity to abuse and assault me. I shall never forget that incident and don't think I deserved to be treated in such a cruel manner. It still makes my blood boil --- my sister Maureen says she also had to eat scraps from the bin. Were we the only two? Probably not, she thinks.

Danny Keaney was by no means one of the school's bad boys and there were plenty of lads larger and older than me who frequently attacked and beat me up in the playground. The favourite method of the attacker was to dish out a dead-leg. Resistance would invite a smack in the chops with a fist. I did not have a reputation for fighting back against bigger boys, but often seemed to be a target.

All I used to think about at that school was how to get back to Norfolk. I didn't even have any idea where it was, or what direction to take.

"How long would it take to walk to Norfolk?" I remember asking one of the teachers. In my mind I was going to escape my miserable Stratford existence back to paradise - and the only way to do it was on foot.

My worst experiences of violence at the school, however, came not from one of our own pupils, or one of the teachers, but at the hands of youngsters from Sir Thomas Jollyffe School which I had attended previously.

Those Catholic boys who passed Thomas Jollyffe School on their way to or from St Gregory's in Henley Street could expect to be attacked, or even stoned, by the Protestant children - even though the attackers were often boys who, out of school, were in my gang and we all lived as neighbours in the "Arab Camp". That seemed to mean nothing. As a Catholic, I was a target and the violence of the attacks had to be seen to be believed.

It was a case of running the gauntlet every day, often watched by parents of the Protestant children but who did nothing to stop it. As we approached the school we could see the kids waiting for us. Brian Harrison was my best mate at the Roman Catholic school and we'd run the gauntlet together – most of the other Catholic children took a longer route down the Birmingham Road to avoid the Thomas Jollyffe, Clopton Road, route to and from St Gregory's.

The stones used to hurt us and sometimes they would draw blood, but we refused to give in to the Protestant boys and I always knew that Brian would stand by me through thick and thin. I'd made up my mind I would do the same for him. Besides, if we took the route down the Birmingham Road route we risked being beaten up by the Park Road kids, who were also a gang.

One day it finally got out of hand. I found myself surrounded by a group of boys from the Thomas Jollyffe School and was knocked to the ground. Mick Simms, one of the Protestant boys, hurled a house brick at my head and split it wide open. I was seriously injured and had about three weeks' treatment at Stratford hospital.

I never forgot what Mick did and as you will read I beat the shit out of him some years later after he attacked me in a Stratford pub with a friend's crutch, when I was in my late teens. Looking back, I think it was the day I finally stood up for myself after years of being on the receiving end of aggression, although some would say I had already become a 'tearaway'.

Mick now lives in France, but when I see him these days we have a drink together. It's an example of childhood brutality forgiven but not forgotten. I think that was the low point of my existence in Stratford and if it hadn't been for Auntie Karfy I would have had no one to turn to. Somehow, she was always there for me and provided the anchor that made our home at least a tolerable place to be.

Girly shoes Keaney...

Having two older sisters posed an unexpected problem in a poor family. My parents expected me to wear their hand-me-downs. I was presented with a Macintosh that had to be done up on the girls' side and a pair of black shoes with no toe caps—boys' shoes had toe-caps. This did not go unnoticed among my tormentors at school and an insulting refrain would be struck up the moment I arrived in the playground.

"Girly shoes Keaney, girly shoes Keaney," they would shout.

I still wasn't an enthusiastic fighter like Fluff, but they would have to have it in such circumstances.

"Whack!" I'd punch my tormentor hard in the mouth.

It inevitably meant another caning from the headmistress.

"Fancy punching poor little Patrick. He wouldn't say boo to a goose," said an angry Miss Harman.

There was no point in telling her what had really happened. She wanted to give me a beating.

My mother used to beat all of us with whatever she could lay her hands on. I would certainly get it if she heard I'd been caned at school. Her favourite weapon was the copper stick used for the washing and she would belt me hard with that.

I'd get it across the knees and the elbows, or the back of the neck. She would also use a metal ladle if she could find it and hit me with that. I have to admit that we all played her up because we knew she had a quick temper. Auntie Karfy would step in and try and stop the beatings if they became too violent.

By now I felt no love for my mother at all, just indifference if not coldness. Both my parents tried to show limited love and affection to their five girls. Sometimes, at home, my sisters would take turns to sit on Jack's knee and he would behave in a relaxed and affectionate manner around them. One year he made an announcement.

"Ok girls, we're all going to the Mop tonight after tea - so go and get your coats. Let's go out with your mother and have some fun in the town."

It very soon became clear that I was not to be included in this family outing to the annual fair in the streets of the town – in fact he did not look at me once or make any reference to me.

When they were ready with their coats on and full of excitement, they went out and the door was shut behind them. I was, of course, feeling extremely miserable at this exclusion, but decided to go to the Mop on my own, even though I did not have any money.

I followed the family at a discreet distance and watched the girls as they ate hotdogs, licked ice cream and bit at toffee apples between rides on the fairground merry-go-rounds. I felt sad, tearful and left out. I just did not understand why. It happened several years in succession, so I dreaded Mop day when it came around.

It was the same when they used to go off to Ireland for a week's holiday to County Leitrim. I was never included in the family party going on the trip across the Irish Sea.

Jack used to say: "You stay at home, guard the house, and keep an eye on the dog."

We didn't have a dog.

Christmas in the Keaney household followed a familiar pattern for years and served to underline that we were a dysfunctional family. Jack would be out most nights during the week before, drinking with his Irish workers from Lumley Saville. On Christmas Day a group of Irishmen, who could not get home to the Republic, would be invited to lunch at our home.

It was Christmas Eve, however, that we dreaded.

Jack would come home particularly late on Christmas Eve and would usually be very drunk. A furious Mabel would accost him for his lack of emotional and financial support and his selfishness. Being pissed, he would lose his temper within minutes. We knew what was going to happen next.

Soon Mabel would start hitting Jack on his face, shoulders and legs, screaming and shouting loudly. This was the signal for us children to retreat to the uncarpeted staircase where, with Auntie Karfy, we were reluctant witnesses to what was happening in the living-room.

The girls would be huddled together bawling their eyes out - and I would sit there staring into space. On the landing, Karfy would try to wrap the few Christmas presents for the children, nearly all from Norfolk, so they would be ready for Christmas morning.

I can never remember Jack or Mabel buying me a Christmas present,(they probably did) but the girls usually had gifts.

"That's a present from me son, Merry Christmas my boy!" were words never uttered by Jack Keaney to me.

My grandmother used to send a big parcel down and there would always be something for me in that. Actually, I had the same thing for five years on the trot. It was a cardboard cut-out owl. Apparently, when you turned out the light its eyes moved. Not much good since in the dark you couldn't see anyhow.

I don't know who used to send it to me. I would also get toy soldiers - and my Uncle Ronnie, who lodged with us for a while, made me a fort for my soldiers one year. We were playing with it in the backyard, just after Christmas, when the Smith lads, David and Terry who had brought their own soldiers, thought it would make a more realistic battle if the fort was put to the torch by the attackers. Before I could stop them, one of the gang found paraffin in the garden shed and tipped it on the fort, followed by a match.

Christmas Day...

When we woke up on Christmas morning the atmosphere between my parents had usually cleared, although there was an uneasy tension which continued until lunchtime when the Irishmen from Lumley Saville started arriving.

The company donated a large cockerel and Christmas pudding to every worker - and some of the guests would bring theirs to augment the Christmas Feast. As the merriment began, the angel Karfy was working hard in the kitchen to give us all a good meal, while Mabel mingled with the male guests in the living room enjoying a tipple.

Some of the guests had been to Mass and all had been drinking since leaving church, so the atmosphere after their arrival became very jolly as the day progressed. Mabel was drinking hard by the time lunch was served by Karfy and by mid-afternoon she did what she was good at and would organise a sing-song around the piano in the front-room, while one of the Irishmen played the fiddle. She may have been pretty useless around the house, but Mabel was an excellent pianist like her mother Nellie.

The party usually degenerated into a piss-up and Irish rebel songs were belted out led by Jack, but no one ever got out of order. With Irishmen in the house you certainly wouldn't be watching television on Christmas Day. There were men at the party who were prepared to talk to and take an interest in me.

One used to give me a pound note every year, so I never felt left out and I entered readily into the spirit of the festivities. It certainly beat the big punch-up and the fight the night before!

I remember my feelings were hurt one year when Jack let them into a secret about his second son Danny.

He announced: "He wasn't born – I pissed him up against a wall and the sun hatched him out!"---that's why I was different then?

Our Christmas parties tended to get even wilder when Uncle Jimmy arrived from Ireland to live with us. He would play a huge part in festivities at Christmas when he was staying with us, especially in leading the sing-songs, keeping a huge word for word repertoire in his head.

He and the other Irish guests would be drinking Potheen. Home-made Potheen is an illegal but traditional Irish spirit traditionally distilled from malted barley, grain or potatoes. It looks like water but there the similarity ends because it's lethal.

In fact, Potheen is one of the strongest alcoholic beverages in the world renowned for its ability to get the drinker intoxicated the morning after drinking it by drinking water - thereby bringing the remaining ethanol back into solution.

For centuries Potheen has been illegal apart from two licensed brands *Knockeen Hills*, and *Bunratty*. Poitín – its Irish name - was generally produced in remote rural areas, away from the interference of the law. If poorly produced it may contain dangerous amounts of methanol and can blind or kill.

That does not put people off and it is popular at weddings and wakes - a large supply of the illegal brew was at hand during Christmas with the Keaneys, shipped from some quiet corner of Ireland for the party.

The Potheen also fuelled the sing-songs in the front room. Many traditional Irish folk songs, such as *The Hills of Connemara* and *The Rare Old Mountain Dew* deal with the subject of Poitín. The song *McIlhatton* written by Bobby Sands and performed by Christy Moore is about a famous distiller of illegally made poitín. Gaelic Storm's song *Darcey's Donkey* on the album *What's the Rumpus?* deals in a humorous way with the consequences of being caught out by the Garda for distilling poitín.

Uncle Jimmy arrives...

The accordion, piano and fiddle-playing Uncle Jimmy came to lodge with us shortly before one Christmas. There wasn't a rebel song he didn't know and he sang them with gusto - no Christmas carols for Jimmy. He was my father's younger brother and was given a job as a bulldozer driver at Lumley Saville to begin with – but was sacked by Jack soon afterwards for being drunk at work. He always felt happier driving people rather than construction machines apparently and got a job as a cabby in Stratford with the Yellow Taxis, a company that was based outside what is now the NatWest Bank. Pissed taxi drivers didn't seem to be much to write home about in the 1950s.

Jimmy was an extrovert with boundless energy and a huge sense of humour who enjoyed playing practical jokes, even if it caused considerable distress to his victim. He eventually got his marching orders from the Keaney home for locking my mother in the windowless brick built coal-shed where she spent six hours in abject misery and mounting frustration. Her presence there was only discovered by me after school, when I heard wild banging on the door coming from the inside calling for someone to let her out. I was the first home from school and released her only to get a good belt from a black-faced mother for laughing---well I thought it was funny.

Uncle Jimmy was well-groomed, dressed smartly, and was handsome, in the Clark Gable style with film star looks. The opposite sex found him handsome and irresistible. This soon resulted in a stream of Stratford beauties knocking on our door including the stunning but devout Miss Scotson, one of the nicer teachers at St Gregory's Roman Catholic School. She was obviously prepared to overlook my uncle's drunken and wayward lifestyle, perhaps intending to reform him into a good Catholic. She didn't last long. His liaisons with the opposite sex tended to be short-lived and I don't remember him ever bringing a woman back to our house, or making any reference or innuendo to sexual adventures.

In the many years that have passed, however, some well preserved Stratford Ladies still ask after him. I am sure he will be standing at the bar in heaven having the "craic." and playing an Angel or two up with a practical joke.

What God gives with one hand, he often takes away with the other. My uncle Jimmy may have been handsome and intelligent, but he was uncontrollably wild and as I've mentioned, already barking mad by his early 20s, a state of mind fuelled by being a dedicated alcoholic partial particularly to Guinness with a whisky chaser when Potheen wasn't available. All the children loved him.

Many a Sunday afternoon during the rest of the year, my sisters and I were taken by an extremely inebriated Uncle Jimmy on a trip to Charlecote Park to see the deer. Swerving from side to side and with us kids hanging out of the car windows and sun roof of Jack Keaney's Riley - which was my father's pride and joy – we'd make drunken progress down the Tiddington Road. These were the days before drink driving carried severe penalties. There were no police squad cars lying in wait with breathalyser kits.

Unfortunately, Jimmy would usually abandon us at Charlecote Park. We'd be left on the side of the road crying, as Uncle Jimmy disappeared in the car to seek out more drink. My mother always refused to blame Jimmy for our upset, because she said he was Irish and that was the sort of thing Irishmen did. We always forgave him, despite being abandoned.

He was always good humoured and even affectionate with us children, but lived on a short fuse and the drink soon caused this to fizz wildly. He'd start teasing and tormenting people. Like most Irishmen he enjoyed a punch-up and was not one to back down.

This was vividly illustrated on my sister Pamela's wedding day in Stratford when he led a procession of cars to the reception in the Red Lion in Bridge Street. I was in the back seat. He missed the turning into the pub car park and stopped his saloon to get out and warn the driver behind that he'd need to reverse up.

In doing so, while leaning into the window of the second car, he lit a cigarette and fell into what Irishmen would describe as a good yarn - with time not being especially important. The driver of the third car, who was not in the wedding procession, eventually became impatient after five minutes of hanging about - and sounded his horn loudly.

Jimmy chose to ignore the first hoot of the horn but this was followed less than a minute later by an even longer and louder hoot.

"Get a bloody move on you sodding Mick - you're holding up the bleeding traffic!" shouted the irate driver who had left his window down. Perhaps he should have exercised more discretion and less valour in the heat of the moment. He would have seen a large dark-haired man strolling up to his car with clenched fists.

"Who the fock are you shouting at you impatient ---t?"

Simultaneously Jimmy landed a hard right punch onto the chin of the driver, who slumped back into his seat for a good sleep. Meanwhile, a traffic queue built up behind the unconscious man in the car. Jimmy drove off, turned back on himself round the traffic island at the top of Bridge Street and parked up at the pub, soon forgetting all about the incident, as he tucked into the food and the booze.

For some reason that defeats me, Pamela and her new husband had agreed to travel with Jimmy in his car after the reception to Luton Airport where they were flying from - to an unknown but exotic destination for their honeymoon. Jimmy was, to say the least, quite legless by the end of the reception - and bride and groom viewed their prospects of ever getting to Bedfordshire as extremely remote.

He got in the car with bride and groom in the back and seemed to sober up a bit, much to the newly-wed's great relief, but he still wasn't able to control the car properly. In fact, as they sped down the MI, swerving all over the road, he proudly showed Pamela the places where he'd been part of the construction team as a bull-dozer driver, sticking his head out of the window and pointing.

They might have made it to Luton Airport had there not been an accident up ahead of them. A lorry carrying crates of full lemonade bottles had been in a collision and overturned – spilling its cargo all over two of the three lanes. The police had closed two of the lanes and the traffic halted as it queued up for a crawl down the third lane - policed by patrol cars with officers directing the traffic.

"What the fock's this!" exclaimed an irritated Jimmy as he approached the hold-up and pulled out impatiently to drive down the lanes which were still blocked by pop bottles and wooden crates. The car narrowly missed one officer who had to leap for his life out of his way. This was followed by mayhem as Jimmy's car hit the cascading bottles of lemonade, scattering glass and fragments of wooden crates everywhere. Pamela remembers the sound of screaming police sirens as their car came to a halt a few yards past the lorry.

Jimmy was hauled off protesting his innocence to the nearest police station and locked up in a cell until the next morning. The police took pity on the weeping Pamela and her husband and arranged for them to be delivered to Luton Airport in time for the flight.

Years later he married a lovely hard-working girl and ended up as landlord of the *Moulders Arms* in Luton, a well known Irish pub. It is hard to imagine a more unsuitable vocation for Uncle Jimmy, but in the times before his health finally gave way he was a legend front of house - and the pub was a well known watering hole for hard drinkers from the Emerald Isle. He is remembered with affection by the entire family.

The swing in our back garden, or where our back garden would have been if Jack Keaney could have been arsed to do anything with it, was given to us by a nice woman called Mrs Bingham one summer in the early-1950s. The Bingham's back garden shared a common fence with part of ours and they were neighbours to the Brook family, whose son Colin was a member of the gang - but who had given me a thrashing when we first moved to Stratford.

The three women, my mother, Mrs Bingham and Mrs Brook, would occasionally get together for a gossip over the garden fence. I remembered her chiefly because of her son David who was six years older than me but quite unlike the other lads of his age in Justin's Avenue. David wasn't part of a gang and didn't beat up younger kids, get into trouble with the police, or get involved with gratuitous violence with other members of his peer group.

A smart boy was David, who did his own thing, and was big and strong enough to make sure no one in Justin's Avenue tried to bully or intimidate him. He came to my attention because of my years of early childhood in Norfolk when I learned to go poaching with my grandfather Fafa. We would occasionally see David setting off towards the Welcombe Hills carrying a powerful air rifle and dressed in waterproofed clothing and boots.

A few hours later he would return with pheasant, hares or rabbits strung over his shoulder which would be eaten by the Binghams, or sold to grateful families at a fair price in the "Arab Camp". Instead of cuffing us across the back of the head when he saw us, David would wave, smile and even chat to us about his poaching. To lower forms of life in the food chain like us, it was astonishing behaviour and he became one of my heroes. I was fascinated by him.

Many years later David left Stratford and my mother was told he had joined the Royal Navy. We occasionally heard reports via our respective mothers about David Bingham's successful naval career in which he became a junior officer, although to be fair he gradually faded from my memory. None of us had any inkling that he would become a Russian KGB agent – going down in history as "the hen-pecked spy".

One day in 1971 there it all was in the *Daily Mirror*. An astonished Colin Brook said to me: "Bloody hell, that's David from next door!"

He was arrested for breaching the Official Secrets Act during his work as a member of the Tactical Advisory Service in Portsmouth, Hampshire. By the time he was 31 years old David had done well, considering he was a boy from a council house and eventually got a commission. He served as a weapons electronics officer, aboard HMS Rothesay, a modified Type 12 Anti-Air Frigate, F107 commissioned in 1960.

It's a fascinating story with a mysterious ending straight out of a John Le Carre novel. He was arrested after handing himself in to the police and owning up to what he had been doing for the previous 18 months. In interviews he provided a list of documents he passed on to the Russians.

Some of the most damaging revelations were said to be of fleet operational and tactical instructions which were to form the basis of an "impending major national exercise".

The documents also revealed the fighting capability of the Royal Navy and outlined its "serious weaknesses" partly in electronic warfare. When he was arrested David, by now the father of four children, initially claimed to have been a KGB spy for years, without his family knowing anything about it.

In a later interview he told MI5 he'd started spying in January 1970 at the suggestion of his wife Maureen after their debts started climbing to £5,000. While David was in hospital with a back problem, Maureen went to the Russian Embassy in London with a note. David was then summoned to a meeting by Russian agents, where he was given vodka and cash.

In the months that followed he took photographs of documents either in his room or his ship cabin, leaving the films in packages around the area. Maureen Bingham was a comfort shopper, a so-called 'shopaholic' and addicted to gambling. David's salary was not sufficiently high to finance his wife's shopping and betting expeditions and this led to his brief career in espionage.

While at the embassy she met with Russian Consular Officials who invited her to return sometime later to a tea-party under the cover of researching a book on "housewives of the world."

Apparently Maureen photographed pages from an exercise book used by her husband for notes and deliberately induced 'camera shake' to ensure that the photographic content of the resultant prints were illegible. She was well aware that the 'intelligence' that she was supplying to the Russians was of no use at all and boasted later that she was "taking them for a ride".

The debts mounted as Maureen Bingham pursued her self-indulgent and excessive shopping. There are suggestions that David had become a big spender too, quite early in his Navy career. It seems that when he returned to his home town he often went to the Theatre and Press Club where he mingled with famous actors such as Peter O'Toole and Dinsdale Landen.

The excessive lifestyle in the early 1970s, coupled with the gambling debts, led to Maureen selling the family car without the knowledge of the Hire Purchase Company that had financed the purchase. There were subsequent meetings with the Russian Naval Attache, Lory Turifmovich, who handed over £2,800 for photographs left in a dead letter box.

It seems it was obvious to David that the Russians knew that the photos supplied by Maureen were of no use whatsoever, but being aware of his position they concluded he would be of use to them in the future. This turned out to be true.

One document supplied by David was, according to the prosecution, "almost beyond price." Eventually he was in so deep he became really scared. He was called to a meeting with his Russian handlers in some woods. David took his son with him and during the meeting Bingham told the Russians that he had had enough and didn't care what they did to him – he didn't have a life any more. At this point a Russian placed a gun to Bingham's head and asked "What about your children's lives?"

On his return, and wishing to protect his children, Bingham approached a senior officer and informed him of the spying activities. Unfortunately David was regarded as such a good character the officer refused to believe what he was hearing - so he was forced to go and tell the Police.

"All I can say is thank God it is over," he told them after he was arrested.

The story printed in the newspapers described David as "the most despicable traitor in the history of post-war espionage." The defence counsel called the case "a story of almost incredible folly" like a "badly written spy novel – "a lurid melodrama of secret assignments, signals that involved leaving empty packets of cigarettes in rural telephone boxes and posting church notices to addresses in Kensington."

David was sentenced to a total of 126 years imprisonment on 12 counts, to run concurrently. This in fact amounted to a sentence of 21 years and Maureen was subsequently arrested and charged with offences under the Official Secrets Act.

At an outrageous press conference at the Russian Embassy she told reporters: "The Russians treated us better than the Royal Navy ever did."

After serving only seven years of the original sentence he was released from gaol. He settled down quietly in the 1980s and rebuilt his life, changing his name and remarrying. He and his new wife ran a small hotel in Bournemouth, Dorset, and he even became the vice-president of the local Conservative Club. The members were probably unaware that he had previously spied for the Russians.

David was still nostalgic for his home town so he found a reason for returning in his new persona. He opened an alternative healing centre in Stratford with his wife, offering therapies at £20 a session. Neither Colin Brook nor I knew him during this latter period in the town, neither did we ever run into him, so we were further shocked when we heard that in February 1997, on a night of severe gales, David had lost control of the car that he was driving near Stratford-upon-Avon and crashed into a tree.

He was killed instantly along with his dog. It is said he was carrying a can of petrol on the front seat, rather than keeping it in the boot. Not everyone in Stratford then, or indeed now, accepted it was an accident. There were rumours David was planning to write his life story to reveal all. That's where I'll leave it. To me and many others who knew him, David will always be that "nice boy" from Hodgson road.

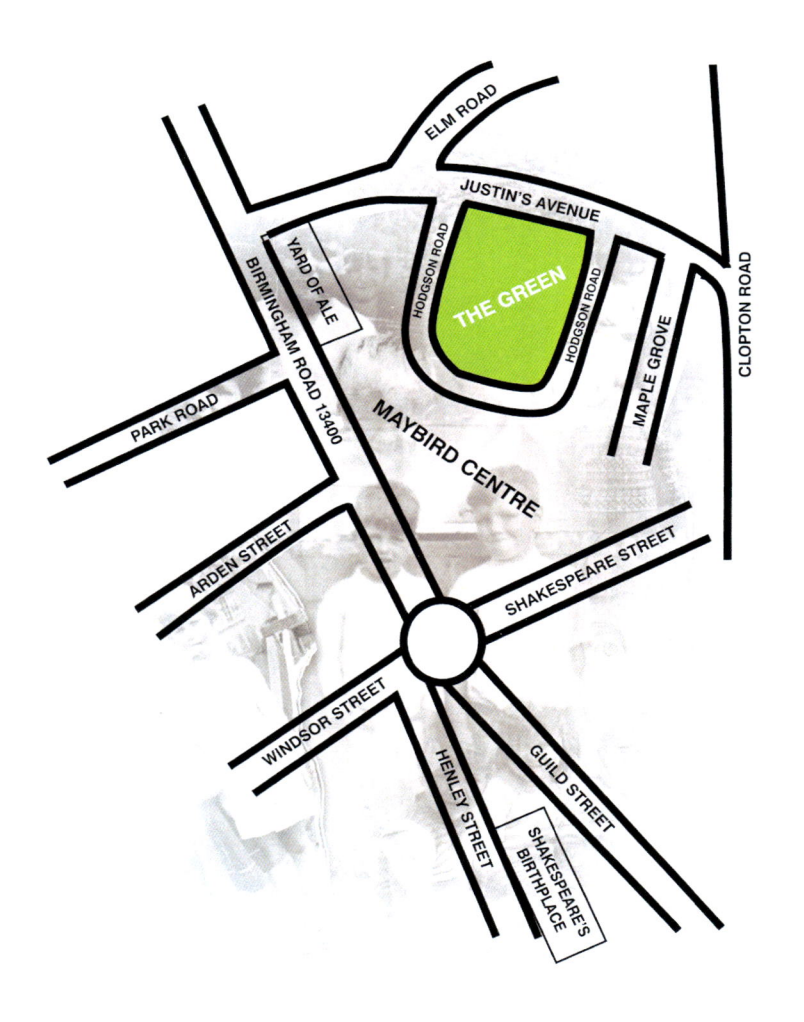

DANNY KEANEY WITH DALE LE VACK

SHAKESPEARE'S CHILDREN

DANNY KEANEY: STRATFORD UPON AVON PSYCHOPATHS R.F.C.

My Rugby career as seen by Terence Parkes the cartoonist 'Larry'

DANNY KEANEY WITH DALE LE VACK

Sean MacDiarmada 'an Irish hero'

SHAKESPEARE'S CHILDREN

Uncle 'Irish' Jimmy liked the craic

DANNY KEANEY WITH DALE LE VACK

At school: A forced smile

SHAKESPEARE'S CHILDREN

Miserable and under guard between Aunty Margaret and Grandmother 'Nellie' on the way back to Stratford at the American War Cemetery in Cambridge

Mum and Dad.
Jack and Mabel on the day they got engaged

SHAKESPEARE'S CHILDREN

Auntie Karfy 'The Angel' at Stratford Mop Fair 1951, pictured with sisters Kathleen, Pamela and brother Cavan

Chapter Four
GROWING UP IN THE ARAB CAMP

About the time Richard Burton was pulling pints late at night behind the bar at the *Dirty Duck* serving Humphrey Bogart and Lauren Bacall with cocktails and signing up - thanks to them - for a 10-picture deal in Hollywood, 'Fluff' Jones and I were trying to grow a runner bean up the arse of "Studger" Evans in Justin's Avenue. A younger and smaller kid, Studger Evans had been getting on our nerves but we decided for some reason we would not give him a good slapping, but try torturing him.

I didn't know any tortures but had remembered about our lodger, my Uncle Ronnie, who'd fought with the Royal West Kent Rifles in the Burma Campaign against the Japanese. He used to say that when the Nips captured British soldiers - and wanted information - they would torture them by growing bamboo shoots up their arse.

"So where are we going to get bamboo shoots from in Justin's Avenue?" asked Fluff dismissively.

"I know!" I said. "Jim Ashfield grows runner beans in his garden. I bet they grow nearly as quickly as bamboo shoots. Why don't we use one of those to grow up Studger's arse?"

"How will we do it?" asked Fluff who was unconvinced about my plan.

"Well, we'll make Studger strip off and sit with a bean growing between his legs and guide it up his arse," I answered triumphantly.

Studger was surprisingly compliant about our plans to torture him in such a violent manner and took off his pants and trousers. He then sat obligingly with the healthy bean plant between his legs and aimed in the direction of his rectum.

"How fast do they grow?" asked Fluff who was anxious to see some action and witness some visible discomfort to the unfortunate Studger.

"Oh it'll be up his arse in no time at all," I reassured Fluff – confident my Uncle Ronnie would not lie to me. We waited patiently for a quarter of an hour to see if the shoots of the bean plant could visibly be seen inching up Studger's backside. Nothing was happening and we began to wonder if it would take all night.

"What are you doing?" asked Jim Ashfield when he arrived on the scene after work.

"We're trying to grow a runner bean up Studger's arse like the Japs did to British soldiers in the War," I explained to Jim, who was visibly unimpressed by my explanation.

"Bugger off boys or I'll cuff you," threatened Jim, anxious to repossess his vegetable plot before there was any damage done to his precious vegetables. Jim was a rare beast in those days – one of the few adults in the immediate vicinity of Justin,s Avenue who seemed to have the inclination to grow anything. Jim was a nice man and didn't get angry when one day I jumped off his shed roof and landed on his expensive glass cloches, smashing them and cutting my legs quite badly on the shards of glass, when playing with his son Malcolm. Jim cleaned up my legs, bandaged them and sent me home with a pat on the head. Some years later a glider crashed on that very same shed killing the pilot.

Studger was from a family of six children; Jenny, Diane, Geoffrey, Maxine, John and of course Studger. Their father Frank was a smart man, as I remember, who always wore a trilby coupled with a nice suit, shirt and tie or cravat. He was Mr. Tom Bird's no-nonsense right-hand man at the scrap yard and he always reminded me of Humphrey Bogart.

Frank and his wife Gwen were good parents and instilled a strong work ethic in their children. Jenny was seen as the "posh" one in the family because it was rumoured she wore knickers every day of the week, not just on a Sunday. Next time I see her I must ask her if it was true.

Tobogganing on the Welcombe Hills…

The Arab Camp boys used to meet the posh kids from Maidenhead Road on the Welcombe Hills and there would always be trouble – like east meets west – especially if it snowed enough in winter long enough for the toboggans to be brought out. They would be wearing their ski jackets and woollen gloves and we'd just have a spare pair of socks to keep our hands warm.

We'd find them sitting astride, or lying on, their factory-made sledges enjoying long and fast runs down the slopes. A toboggan for us, likely as not, would be a car bonnet nicked from Bird's scrap-yard.

Sad to say now, but they had to have it for being posh and also for having the nerve to take the piss out of our winter sports equipment. Many a toboggan from Maidenhead Road had the firewood axe put through it, to teach them a lesson. Some of us carried an axe for chopping up wood that we'd collect for fires at home.

I can't remember any of the names of the posh kids except for Stephen Whittaker. I always had a grudging respect for him because he would always stand his ground and fight back. Later in life Stephen had a part in the film *Kes* and went on to have a successful career in acting and working on films and TV as a producer.

We'd meet the Maidenhead Road kids again sometimes on Saturday mornings when the Picture House in Greenhill Street put on children's films. The Arab camp boys would buy the sixpenny tickets and the posh kids sat together for collective protection in the shilling seats upstairs.

Before the start of the screening the posh kids could afford to buy bags of sweets which they'd munch through the performance, but we'd prefer – being hungry - a lovely hot loaf from the baker's shop, over the road from the cinema. We'd scoop out the white fluffy bread and eat it and then fashion the outside crust of the loaf into a pair of boxing gloves. If the film got boring we'd charge upstairs and attack the posh kids in the expensive seats. A cottage loaf boxing glove delivered to the lug-'ole of a posh kid was all part of the Stratford on Avon Saturday morning's entertainment.

Most of the time, however, our aggravation was focused upon other working class kids from the council estates in Stratford. An exception to this was the poor demented son of Sir Thomas Beecham who lived at Clopton House. We had no idea what was wrong with him except that he looked dangerous, because to us he was huge, like an ugly bear. His minder used to leave him alone in the garden to play. He was chained to a stake by his ankle to prevent him wandering away. We had only seen dogs chained like that.

The poor chap was, of course, intellectually challenged and deserved nothing but kindness and consideration from his peer group - rather than teasing and unkindness which is what he got from the wicked mob from Justin's Avenue.

We were cruel bastards, but I suppose we were too young to understand what was wrong with the chap. We called him "the mad kid". He soon became a target for our abuse; especially since he was the son of a famous and eminent man – although none of us knew anything about Sir Thomas or his international musical career as the world's leading conductor. The great man was regularly seen driving his open-top car up the drive between the pillars of the great house.

I was in a group of kids that one day crept into the garden of Clopton House. Some were armed with air rifles and concealed behind a shrubbery. "The mad kid" was chained to the stake and gazed vacuously about 30 yards away into the far horizon. He did not hear us coming. We had gone there to shoot him up the arse. I am thankful now that I didn't own an airgun then.

Someone had seen a film with musketeers firing at charging cavalry in two ranks – like in the "squares" at Waterloo and one bigger kid who fancied himself as a future NCO ordered an organised fusillade to be unleashed upon Master Beecham with deeply unfortunate intensity upon his backside.

"Front rank fire! Second rank, fire!" ordered the big kid. He began dancing around the lawn like a demented Dervish, bellowing like a wounded bull as each pellet struck home, inflicting stabs of pain upon the rear part of his anatomy. Eventually the roars of distress attracted the attention of his minder who rushed out of the house to investigate its cause. The gang dispersed in good order without being chased.

The adrenalin had kicked in and we were on a high for a while after the adventure. A sense of anti-climax gradually replaced the exhilaration. We were bored after such a dangerous incursion into the inner sanctum of Clopton House, but weren't sure what to do after that – or where to go. Then someone had a good idea.

"David Huckfield has started a zoo in his back garden. Let's go and see him."

We walked back to Justin's Avenue and knocked on the front door of the Huckfield home.

"It'll cost you sixpence to come in," said David.

I had to borrow the money but we were all intrigued to see what David had collected for his zoo and we filed into his garden with a keen sense of anticipation. It turned out to be the second anti-climax of the day. The zoo comprised a jam-jar with three moths in it. I demanded my money back but I don't think I got it.

Poor David Huckfield died tragically a couple of years later. One of the pastimes of the gangs was to lay pennies on the railway line at Bishopton, jump clear at the last moment and then scrutinise to what extent the coin had been flattened. This time it was a game of chicken too far.

The unfortunate David jumped clear of the steam train approaching on the line where his pennies had been laid - but had failed to notice there was another steam locomotive approaching from the other direction, going towards Stratford.

He was hit by the moving train he hadn't seen and was killed instantly. I was not there but news filtered back to me about the tragedy. Needless to say the dare devil game continued despite the sad end to David Huckfield whose young life was cut short in such a violent manner.

A bizarre sexual experience...

Sex had reared its ugly head a few months earlier when I was still in Stratford and not yet eight years old.

"Danny, have you ever seen a fanny?" asked Fluff.

"No, but some "big boys" said they're really nice," I replied.

"Well, if you want to see one Mrs X will be up Welcombe at two o'clock. She's going to show us her fanny."

Mrs X was middle-aged and had a reputation for being very friendly, and also had a reputation for hanging out with boys of our age. We went up to the Welcombe Hills after lunch - and sure enough she arrived soon afterwards.

"Lie on your back lads," she ordered and we all lay obediently on the grass. She was wearing a pair of white shorts with no knickers, pulled her shorts to one side and stepped over us.

"Fucking 'ell Fluff, run quick!" I shouted, getting up and fleeing the scene followed by my pal.

We ran up towards the Round Tower.

"What's the matter? What's the matter?" Fluff was yelling. I didn't stop until we got to the top of the hill.

"What's the matter?" Fluff yelled again.

"Fucking 'ell, didn't you see that?" I shouted.

"What?" he asked.

"She had a fucking rat coming out of her arse!" I shouted.

"That was her fanny you Twat," Fluff replied – deeply frustrated because he hadn't had time to take a closer look at Mrs X's anatomy. I was that shook-up I had to go home and read my Noddy book — I bet Noddy and Big Ears didn't know people like that. My Aunty Karfy noticed my discomfort and remarked that "it looks like you've seen a ghost"--- 'er not quite.

Mrs X was quite notorious in the Arab camp. During one November in preparation for Guy Fawke's Night, when the gang was a bit older, we built a bonfire on the green and put a den at the centre of it.

Mrs X enticed some of the older boys inside for sex games and gave a catapult to each lad who obliged her. I suppose it was better than sex education at school. I didn't go in there myself because I was too young and didn't really understand what was going on, although I did want one of her catapults.

There were some strange adults around at that time. One bloke I won't name would hang around with us and when we broke into Bird's forbidden pit – which we often did because we couldn't resist it - he used to follow us seven and eight year olds down there.

"When you want to have a pee come and do it on my hands," he'd say. I think we were lucky really because there was no resultant physical sexual abuse directed at us from this repulsive character.

"Why does he want us to do it?" we would ask one another, in all innocence. It wasn't until later that we realised the strange bastard must have been a pervert.

By the time we were 10 and 11 the age of masturbation had kicked in as we became aware of our sexuality.

There was a tree in the Welcombe Hills - still standing today - that in our era was known as "the wanking tree." It was so called because some of the bigger lads used to climb high into its branches and beckon us younger ones to follow. Then they'd show us how to masturbate. Why we were expected to climb up a tree to do it remains a mystery to this day, but I cannot walk past that tree without recalling those innocent days of sexual experimentation. I often point the tree out to the wife when we walk past it---but I get no reply---I have a feeling that she thinks I'm slightly mad.

Bird's pit was a veritable playground; the kind of thing modern kids, obsessed with computer games, could only dream of having just up the road. It was packed with the hulks of tanks, armoured cars and other vehicles which were waiting to be broken up for scrap by Tom Bird's company.

The old man and his workers tried hard to prevent us from trespassing down there, but being determined young rascals we'd usually manage to find a way in. One morning I climbed through the open turret of a tank and dropped inside.

One of the lads, probably Fluff, thought it would be a joke to shut the lid down, but when he'd done so he could not lift it up again. I was trapped inside in the darkness on a hot day. There was no way out. There was silence and no sound from outside because the gang had run off in panic to find help. I started to cry.

"I'm going to die," I sobbed.

It must have been half an hour before help arrived and trapped in the dark, sweating in the heat, I became extremely frightened. Then there was a commotion from outside, followed by talking, and the sounds of tools hammering on the side of the turret.

"Don't worry son, we'll soon get you out!" the reassuring voice of a fireman called to me. It calmed me down and I felt exhilarated when the sky suddenly appeared at the top of the turret and beams of sunlight replaced darkness. My tear-stained face was grinning with relief when my head appeared into the daylight.

"Fresh air," I murmured.

Suddenly, the side of my head was clubbed by a huge fist and I tumbled off the top of the tank, onto the ground, pursued by an adult figure. I looked up and saw the angry face of Tom Bird staring down at me, imminently about to land another 'four-penny' one across the back of the head.

"Don't you ever dare come onto my property again you bad boy," he shouted and may have been restrained by one of the firemen from giving me a real hiding that I would not forget in a hurry.

The rest of the gang had fled at this outburst of rage from Tom Bird, who was quite capable of giving us all a good thrashing. Knowing kids were trespassing there must have made him continually mad at us. Two sides of the yard, which used to be a clay quarry, had mini cliff faces which many a child hurtled down injuring themselves badly, including my sister Ann.

Shortly afterwards the famous Stratford bricklayer Jack Bloxham set the world brick-laying record when he built a series of brick-built pillars around Bird's scrap yard. Fixed metal fencing added to the height of the screening.

One day we found a box of hand grenades in the scrap yard which weren't armed and were used for throwing practice. We shared them out and with grenade in hand I went into Mrs Jessop's shop on the way home. The shop soon emptied with shoppers falling over each other to escape the boy who was tossing a grenade in the air and catching it.

Mr and Mrs Jessop had fled to their store room for safety and I stood alone in the quiet shop, meanwhile I took advantage of the empty shop and helped myself to pocketful of walnuts. The silence was finally broken by the voice of Mrs Jessop from the safety of the store room.

''Danny! She called with a shrill and terrified edge to her voice.

"Yes Mrs Jessop," I replied.

"Keep away from my new bacon slicer," she pleaded. She wasn't bothered about me getting blown to smithereens, she just didn't want me anywhere near her expensive and shiny new bacon slicer if the grenade exploded --- but I of course knew it couldn't. That little innocent incident resulted in another good thrashing.

One thrashing I didn't deserve from my mother was over a packet of biscuits. I had saved my bus fare for a week by walking to school in order buy a packet of my favourite McVities Digestive biscuits, which I bought on Friday afternoon from Fields shop at the bottom of Justin's avenue. I took them home hidden up my jumper, safe from the ''big kids'' up Justin's Avenue only to be accused, when I arrived home, of stealing them by my mother. She snatched them off me, gave me a good belting and sent me to bed.

A popular activity was catching wild ducks on the River Avon and selling them for the table to grateful families in Justin's Avenue for a few pence. We used to do it around the Bancroft Gardens and the theatre. We'd put a piece of bread on a large fish hook while pretending to be fishing. The ducks literally queued up to gobble the bread and they were hauled in and quickly dispatched.

One day a large drake (male duck) took off with the bread hooked down his beak and was flying straight above the heads of theatre goers as we tried to reel it in---it was not a pretty spectacle.

We were admonished by several plump Americans.

"What the hell d'yer think yer doin boys?" asked one.

"It's an old Stratford tradition," we explained innocently and politely to our trans-Atlantic cousins.

"Fuck 'em!" We said to one another.

My mother used to hit me if she heard I'd been in trouble in the town or at school and I think she sought to curb my somewhat unruly behaviour by sending me to piano lessons.

She could have taught me herself, of course, because she was a dab-hand on the old ivories but I don't think she had any inclination to do so. There was a piano teacher at the top of Maple Grove and I was sent with my sisters to have lessons. I had one tutorial but did not like it and realised that the only way of getting out of going to this woman's house would be to break a window. As I left I smashed it with a stone. After that, she wouldn't have me anywhere near the place---job done.

During the winter, my sister Pamela and I would be sent to fetch a bag of coal from the yard in Birmingham Road using the old family pram. Our way of paying for it was to load the pram with empty beer bottles from home (plenty of them) and take them to the Flowers Brewery bottle-yard further down the road towards town.

We'd get a chit stating how many bottles we'd delivered, and then present that to the office to collect the cash. We bought the coal with the bottle money. One day we were pushing my bag of coal home when I was set upon by some bigger kids from Park Road who gave me a slap and made off with some of the coal.

I never went that way again. Looking back, I think it was a sobering reminder of the level of poverty for many people living in the north of Stratford in the 1950s---mugged for a few lumps of coal. Another reminder was the potato picker's lorry which used to park at the junction of Hodgson Road and Justin's Avenue to pick up the mothers, some with young children, to do a day's hard graft in the potato fields around Stratford.

They clambered onto the back of the lorry, wearing their head scarf and warm coat - and carrying their enamel buckets – it was another indication of the austere times and lack of household money in those years. Those local working class women were made of stern stuff and more than did their bit to put food in their children's mouths.

It was the era of the Teddy Boys and Stratford had two Teddy Boy haunts. One was the Barbecue Café in Greenhill Street and the other, owned by stock-car racing hero Ellis Ford, was the Primrose Café, where the Natwest Bank is now situated. Our gang was too young to patronise either café, or venture into the members' only night club that Ellis ran above the café.

However, the memories of Teddy Boys with their quiff-combed greasy hair, side-burns and DA cut at the back of the neck, will never fade. Some wore their drainpipes and long Edwardian jackets in rich colours such as powder blue and maroon – all wearing their thick crepe sole brothel creeper shoes. Many of them fancied themselves as hard boys, but Ellis and his right hand man "Lucy" Loughran, would have no truck with trouble in his coffee bar and the "Teds" knew it.

Ellis had a bad limp caused by a World War Two Mosquito crash but it never stopped him throwing out trouble-makers. He did it with a smile on his face. It seems only yesterday that the Teddy Boy cars, Ford Zodiacs, Zephyrs, Consuls were parked outside in the street. Ellis drove a Ford Mustang, the real thing. He died in 2002.

Jimmy Keaney worked for the yellow taxi company, whose office was next to the Primrose, and doubtless patronised it. He would not have been remotely intimidated by Teddy Boys and preferred alcohol to expresso coffee, but may have used the café to meet young ladies. We'll never know.

Hanging Robert Sharlott...

The argument still rages today – do violent films and DVDs breed violence when watched by impressionable people like children? History shows us that violent films or DVDs do breed violence.

In our day it was the comics that encouraged inappropriate behaviour. Many were full of cheaply illustrated Second World War stories, which cast the Germans as villains and the Allies as good guys.

We read them avidly in the 1950s and were deeply influenced by the heroics of soldiers fighting on our side. I remember one was called *Battler Briton*. We soon came to loathe the Germans, referred to in these comics as the Krauts, Square Heads or the Hun. We hunted down potential Nazi enemies and sought ways to exact our own revenge, even though the war had been over for more than 10 years.

We decided, for example, to hang Robert Sharlott having heard a rumour he was of German descent. In fact, his forefathers had been French – and France was Britain's ally. We blamed Robert, nonetheless, for all the Nazi war crimes. We thought he should be punished, anyway, for what the Germans had done.

Thankfully, he survived his terrifying ordeal, although a little longer in the neck. First we frogmarched him, more as a prank, to a suitable-looking tree in the Welcombe Hills and slung a rope over a large branch. We put the rope around his neck and stood him on a five-gallon drum.

It was only supposed to be a mock execution but one of the gang kicked the drum away and Robert was swinging for several moments before we cut him down. The lad took it surprisingly well, considering he had a red weal round his neck for several weeks. Mrs Sharlot came to our house later that day to complain, and I received a good hiding from my mother.

Stratford Cattle Market was another favourite playground. One day we were on the roof of the café and it gave way beneath our combined weight. We must have fallen 12 feet to the floor in a cloud of thick dust and after the air had cleared we noticed we had dropped at a spot next to the farmers' bar which was stocked with bottled beer and cigars.

Pretending we were hard up farmers, moaning about the weather and wondering why our daughters didn't have boy friends, we sat around the table drinking the beer and puffing away on the cigars - until one by one we started to be sick from inhaling the smoke. Finally we realised we couldn't get out because it was locked, so we hd to climb out again through the hole in the roof.

There's no doubt that as we became older, the cheekier we were to authority. When he was thirteen or fourteen Studger Evans managed to acquire a battered old "scrambler" motorbike and it was his pride and joy to ride it around the fields in the Welcombe Hills. There was a high-landed field in front of Clopton House, Sir Thomas Beacham's home, which was Studger's favourite location for opening out the throttle on his machine.

"You can borrow my air gun with a load of pellets if you like – and we'll have a "go" on your motorbike," Fluff said to Studger who could not resist a "go" with Fluff's gun. We sat astride the machine and let rip across the field with me on the back and Fluff at the front steering.

After ten minutes a police Land Rover turned up in the field. Someone in the big house – perhaps Sir Thomas himself – had complained that two idiots on a motorbike were disturbing the peace. They pulled up at the side of us as we were riding it at about thirty miles an hour and one of the coppers leaned out of the window.

"Stop now," he ordered.

"Fuck off, I'm not stopping," Fluff shouted back, with me sitting on the back like a right dickhead, unable to do anything. Fluff opened up the throttle and charged on, with the Land Rover in pursuit and one of the coppers still shouting, with his head hanging out of the window.

Studger at the side of the field watched horrified at prospect of his precious machine being damaged.

"Stop that motorbike now!" the policeman was shouting sternly.

"Fuck off!" Fluff called back.

To rub it in Fluff suddenly leapt onto the saddle standing on it like a stunt rider and stretched out his left leg so it trailed behind him like a ballerina. At this point I was beside myself with laughter, but the police Land Rover remained on our tail with the copper in the passenger seat still bawling at us.

"Fuck off!" Fluff was singing it this time, taunting the policemen.

He then decided we'd make a run for it and so we hurtled down the field towards the back of some garages, where there was a hedge and a ditch. Unfortunately, we were going too fast and couldn't stop to get off and make our getaway.

Fluff hit the brakes, which tipped us off, but the machine kept going for another 20 yards before disappearing into the ditch, hitting the back of the garages with a loud clonk.

Miraculously, we were not hurt but had by now been collared by the policemen, who were laughing and not inclined to arrest us. An enraged Studger then crept up behind us unseen and shot Fluff in the arse with the airgun at point blank range. So the police jumped on him instead, and left us alone.

When we were bored and had nothing else to do, we used to stage a biggest right "bollock" competition. Fluff thought that one up because he knew he was going to win. Many years later, when Fluff and I were team mates at Stratford Rugby Club, the same competition was re-enacted with new participants. Fluff won again.

A ginger-haired freckled-faced boy by the name of Steven Edkins, who was two or three years older than me, was certainly my nemesis in and around Justin's Avenue and the Clopton Road area. Without fail, every time we crossed paths, I got well and truly hammered. But my worst nightmare, on being pinned to the ground by two or three larger lads, was to hear the words "go and get the dog shit."

Oh no! Not the dog shit treatment! They would bring it on a stick and try and force the dog turd into your mouth. Why would children do that? Where had they seen that being done before? Was it another old Stratford tradition?--the "Arab camp lollipop".

On one occasion, where the Clopton Road meets the Birmingham Road, Steve was giving me such a beating that a passing motorist stopped his car and intervened. I was off like a young hare.

Not all the boys were idiots, who thought of nothing else but violence. The Keenan brothers – Sid and Liam – concentrated on their football. Both were gifted players who went on to play for the town. Sid is now the highly regarded President of Stratford Town Football Club. The Clark brothers Neville and Barry were also gifted footballers who went onto play for the town. My brother Cavan married their sister Sandra and the Clarks' football genes were passed down to their sons.

For most of us, however, being in a gang was the only form of protection, and it produced a form of comradeship that we remembered for years afterwards. I remember one August night we camped up in tents on the Welcombe Hills in preparation for an early morning attack upon the Park Road gang.

We were armed with catapults and bows and arrows, and as our camp fire burned and the stars blazed in the night sky above, we discussed the form and nature of our coming assault upon the hated enemy. It was perhaps just as well we couldn't find anyone to attack next morning.

We might well have been spooked out that night had we known that ghosts were probably moving among us. Just over 300 years before on several nights in late August 1651, Oliver Cromwell had sent 30,000 men of the New Model Army to camp in the hills - while he and his senior officers stayed in the town and on one night dined at what is now The Dirty Duck.

The Army embarked the following week by river to Evesham and then on to Worcester where it defeated and annihilated the Scottish army of Prince Charles, later to become King Charles II.

We must have camped that night on exactly the spot where the 17th century soldiers had made their bonfires and set up their tents.

An end to the horror story...

At the age of 11 my horrific years at St Gregory's at last came to an end and the following term I was sent to Hugh Clopton Secondary School on the Alcester Road, where I spent 12 months.

I was beaten up on my first day of term by older kids, which to be fair was a fate shared by all the new boys. I can't remember the names of my tormentors. I tried fighting back once or twice, but it didn't work to do that. They were too big and strong.

The old joke about having your head stuck down the toilet actually happened to me and to crown that someone flushed it. During my time there I remember getting six strokes of the cane across the arse from the headmaster Mr Darlow, which caused welts across my backside as thick as my finger. I can't remember what it was for, but it certainly wasn't for watching the girls play netball - which was a caning offence inflicted upon some of the older boys. I cannot in truth remember much about my year at Hugh Clopton. The problem was I did not like school and was always bored with the lessons. Indeed, I had no interest in studying whatsoever, as my end of term reports usually reflected.

We played some football - at which I did not excel - and I can remember the twins John and Mick Collet. They were good footballers who both went on to play for the town and these days are playing good golf. I had one or two punch ups with John and Mick, but being identical twins you could never tell which one it was.

I didn't make any close friends among my fellow pupils at Hugh Clopton but took away memories of certain teachers like 'Killer' Greswick who was the woodwork master. He would give you a good hammering if you played up, and I remember the French teacher Fred Earnshaw who later became the Mayor of Stratford. He was something of a character and liked by the pupils.

It was hard to avoid the conclusion later in life, when we look back, that those who went to Hugh Clopton Secondary Modern School were already regarded as second-rate by the education authority. They had come to the conclusion that the secondary modern pupils were unlikely to succeed in the academic world, and therefore should not be considered seriously for possible scholastic achievement and higher education.

We were 11-year-olds but it had already been decided we would, at best, fulfil the pre-ordained vocational role of tradesmen. It was a major step forward for the working classes when comprehensive schools came into being 10 years later because they tried to optimise educational opportunities for all.

Today, Stratford High School, the successor to Hugh Clopton, has a thriving sixth form which feeds the universities and its pupils play a significant role in the cultural life of the town.

It is very satisfying to note that many former pupils of my generation at secondary modern school became highly successful businessmen in later life, with little thanks to what they had experienced educationally at Hugh Clopton.

There we were, less than a mile from the most famous theatre in the world, and about the same distance from the birthplace of the greatest English writer and poet – but I cannot remember ever being taught one word about him successfully - or taking part in any classroom discussion about William Shakespeare and the plays.

Occasionally we were given passages from one of the plays to read aloud in class, but to our ears it was meaningless crap, because no attempt was made by the teacher to explain what they meant or their context to our language. Significantly, our secondary education was taking place during a golden age of the theatre in Stratford, when some of the world's top actors were performing there.

This is not to say I would have been remotely interested in the Bard at that time. I was, after all, an empty-headed 11-year-old; but William Shakespeare and his plays, the magnificent theatre on the Avon, and the world famous actors and actresses who "strutted" their stuff upon its stage, lived on a different planet, to which only the privileged kids at King Edward VI Grammar School ever had occasional access.

By the way, I am not against grammar schools and I'm proud that ours – both for the boys and girls - have teacher-pupil ratios equivalent to Eton College and achieve academic results right at the top of the secondary education league.

However, I'd be interested to know how many of my contemporaries from Justin's Avenue in the 1950s and early 1960s ever go now to performances by the Royal Shakespeare Company, despite all the positive efforts of Peter Hall, and in more recent times Greg Doran, to make the theatre a place for everyone.

All my life I have felt alienated from it somehow, still imbued with the idea that it excludes the "great unwashed" like us. It is, of course, an inferiority complex. We feel that we would not understand, or appreciate, the work of William Shakespeare because we have had insufficient education.

Yet the Bard was our kinsman in many ways, a poacher too like me they say, and we people, brought up in working class Justin's Avenue, are surely his children.

I admit that I am yet to go to a Royal Shakespeare Company performance because of that feeling of exclusion. The years are slipping by and every few months I say to myself that I intend to change things. I will one day become a theatre-goer and am always receiving invitations to go from friends like the actor Robert Lister and his wife Pat.

Chapter Five
THE MAN WITH A GUN IN A TREE

The moon was out
The night was bright
'Twas there for all to see
'We'll do well tonight – I know my boy'
Said the man with a gun in a tree

We crept about so nothing heard
For that's the way to be
'You follow me and look and learn'
Said the man with a gun in a tree

A twig would snap, the birds took flight
And he'd stop and look at me
'Tread lightly boy or we will fail'
Said the man with a gun in a tree

The years went by and my brave soldier he died
Just one that fought for the free
'You're on your own, don't let me down'
Said the man with a gun in a tree

At the ruined church where pheasants sleep
I'm alone with gun in hand
In moonbeam's veil, a figure stands
And I shake from head to knee
A smile and a wave – and I wave back
It was the man with a gun in a tree

My grandfather's death left a void in my life when I returned from Stratford to live in Norfolk in 1959 following his death in 1958. I missed Charlie my soul mate and remember how sad I felt in his last months when he was so withered and drawn in his face. I dreamed about him one night after he had gone, and the poem just seemed to write itself the following morning.

You could see the marked difference in him and all his energy had been dissipated, despite sitting in the sun for hours in an old deckchair in his allotment near his Flemish Giant grey rabbits, which I kept after he'd gone. The Woodbine would still be attached to his lower lip even when he talked to me. We'd chat and he'd tell me about his time as a prisoner-of-war in Germany.

He used to tell me and my sisters that in the camp at Dulmen, the Germans would serve up a big pot of soup stew every day and each prisoner had to line up in a queue to get a bowl of it. He'd tell us about the huts where they slept and electrified barbed wire fences that kept them from escaping. But the story about the stew is the one I remember clearly.

"The trouble is if you were first in the line they used to throw you in the pot," he told us kids and we half-believed him.

Sometimes I wondered after he'd gone whether he was watching me from up in heaven. At night, on my own, poaching under a starlit sky, I could feel his presence around me and sensed his goodwill towards me.

Uncle Sonny would come poaching with me occasionally but there was no one to take the place of Fafa, especially on the dark cold nights when the solitude would bring with it a feeling of melancholy, despite the anticipation of shooting and trapping rabbits and game birds.

I continued to keep Nellie's larder well stocked up and to use Fafa's rusty single-barrel twelve-bore for the next few years. Eventually, even I began to realise it was becoming unsafe and reaching the end of its life.

I was by now working part-time for 'Charlo' English on the farm - while still at secondary school - so I was able to save up to buy a new gun. The old gun was sent off to one of Charlie's brothers to repair it – but I never got it back. The first gun I bought of my own cost £15 and I had to pay 10 shillings a month to buy it. It helped me to become a very successful poacher. Fafa would have been proud of me - and those thousands of hours when he allowed me to accompany him out poaching had paid off.

Fafa, always having a sense of humour, might have found the way his wake turned out to be highly amusing. After the funeral some of the guests came back to the house. My father, never the most sensitive of men, turned it into an Irish wake with everyone drinking beer and getting pissed up.

A cup of tea and a piece of cake in the Norfolk tradition was not enough for Jack Keaney. He invited his Irish mates to Saxlingham Nethergate and they got stuck into the booze, getting louder and louder. It was a typical clash of cultures between the Roman Catholicism of Jack's world and the restrained Anglican tradition of Norfolk villagers.

I remember Nellie my grandmother bursting into tears, because she thought such raucous behaviour was disrespectful to her beloved Charlie's memory. She felt people were having a laugh, like being at a wedding reception, when the atmosphere should have been sad, restrained and respectful.

A new school in Norfolk...

I was now able to resist my parental demands and became adamant I was not going back to Stratford and Hugh Clopton Secondary Modern School. They agreed without too much of a fight and allowed me to stay in Norfolk at the start of my second year of secondary education in 1959. Perhaps they thought that with Charlie gone, I could fill his place in the house and be of assistance to Nellie.

I was sent to Long Stratton Secondary Modern School just up the road from the village. It was, of course, far more rural than Hugh Clopton Secondary and there was certainly nothing like the level of violence there.

Norfolk was certainly a different world to the horrors of Justin's Avenue. The children at the school were much nicer and more innocent, certainly not prone to violent behaviour.

There was a ginger-haired boy called Danny Ryan who used to give me a good slapping, but gradually I became more of a leader than a victim, especially when I became involved in sport like cricket and athletics, especially cross-country running.

I had no interest, however, in academic studies and my lack of application began to bring me into conflict with the teachers.

Here are some examples from my uninspiring school reports which apart from English and reading are much in need of improvement.

(PE and Games) *Much improved with football but needs more self control.* (Somewhat prophetic)

(Music) *It's a pity he seems happiest at the bottom.*

(History) *Work and conduct needs to be improved.*

(General report) *Most unsatisfactory! He seems intent on getting into trouble whenever possible and has not sufficient self-discipline to behave himself when he is not under supervision. His final term has been largely what one would expect from a boy who has no great interest in school but has been successful at times.*

I still have this fear of desks in a row. I hate them. I loathe sitting in a room at a desk or at a table and having to learn something. Unless, that is, it is something I want to learn. Then

I'll go for it. I wouldn't say I shone at anything, but I surprised both myself and the teacher in metal work class when the firing pin broke on Fafa's old shotgun.

I sat down and figured out how I could replace it in the metalwork class. I filed it out of a piece of metal in a vice. Then I put it in the gun myself and it worked perfectly. I suppose I had learned how to do the job because I wanted to do it.

Looking back I think I was wild, rebellious and anti-authority without perhaps realising I was like that. I suppose also that the tough years in Stratford had conditioned me. I had become a defiant spirit. Who was it that said that rules are for the guidance of wise men and the obedience of fools?

There was a house point system at the school and if you lost a certain number of house points you had the cane on a Monday morning before assembly. You were called out to the headmaster's office and had to bend over his desk and get a whacking of two or three strokes. It was always the same three or four individuals every Monday morning without fail.

"The following will report to the headmaster's office right away. Jarrett, Keaney, Ward."

The whacking really hurt and there would be tittering from the other pupils when we emerged at assembly, holding our arses in pain, but we still carried on doing it, losing house points.

Full-time on the farm...

Eventually, at the age of 15, I left the school and started work full-time for 'Charlo'. I was lucky on several occasions not to get sacked because I really was quite wild, even though I didn't know

I was wild.

I remember his first combine harvester which was a six foot cut. Against his better judgement, 'Charlo' allowed his young labourer to drive the brand new machine; it was his pride and joy.

Once I got behind the controls a feeling of power surged into my head. I started it up and immediately raced off down the lane at an inappropriate speed before trying to get the machine into the cornfield.

I misjudged the open gate because of the speed I was travelling at and turned too quickly - colliding with the sturdy gate-post causing a terrible crunching sound. The front of the combine was badly buckled. 'Charlo' went ape-shit. He had trusted me and I had let him down.

I continued to work for the English family for over two years until I was nearly 18 and loved the work through the seasons of the year - just as old Charlie had. I felt I was born to farm and although I had become a wild and sometimes irresponsible sod, I did take pride in my work, whether it was digging ditches, fencing, milking, tending the livestock or ploughing and drilling the land. My greatest joy at the weekend was in taking my rabbits to Norwich Market.

I specialised in Flemish Giants which was the same breed that Fafa had kept. They were a meat rabbit, rather than pet rabbit and I could get a good price selling at the market to butcher shops. I used to be happy with £1 a rabbit and I would take a dozen to market in a crate in my friend Bryan Ward's car. He came from the same village and used to sell goats which stank the car out – but not as badly as him. Mind you he did marry Murveen, the best looking girl in the village

I'll never forget the day Tom Simmons castrated a pig the size of a Labrador with his penknife while my uncles Cecil and Pinky held it down. Pigs are meant to be castrated when they are a few days old, but we had never got round to it - and this one needed fattening up for market.

"Won't take a minute Bor," Tom assured us as he sharpened the blade of his pocket knife on a stone. We thought old Tom had been doing this for years – at least that's what he said and we believed him. In fact, he'd never castrated a pig in his life and finally admitted it just before he started. My uncles were fed up with holding down the pig and told him impatiently to get on with it anyway. I'll never forget what happened next – in fact it made my eyes water.

He cut, he twisted and he pulled while the pig squealed so loud you could hear it half a mile away. The testicles were eventually freed from their cord with a loud squelching noise and Tom held them up proudly so we could see them. They were the size of a couple of large pears – too large for Nellie to fry up for tea. The poor pig rushed back into its sty and buried itself under a pile of straw. It didn't come out for two weeks and when it did it was as lean as a greyhound. We eventually fattened it up and ate it.

Harvest time remained a joy. I sometimes wondered, though, whether Charlie had been smitten with the same wanderlust - and then it occurred to me that at my age he'd gone off to fight a war in France.

My beloved Norfolk – I was getting bored with it! I could hardly believe it. I continued to keep Nellie's larder well stocked up with game and in the poaching season I was out perhaps two nights a week shooting or trapping. By now I had grown tall and sturdy and was confident of my own strength, but not a troublemaker or even a heavy drinker.

I felt something was missing in my life – quiet nights down the pub, watching TV in the cottage kitchen, or roaming the countryside with my gun at night was no longer sufficient to satisfy me. I began to crave peer group companionship which the village did not give me – neither did it yield the sight and shape of any attractive girls.

It gradually dawned on me that I was missing Stratford – the town that I had learned to loathe as a child was now beckoning me to come back at last. There were good times to be had there I told myself – and lots of girls.

DANNY KEANEY WITH DALE LE VACK

Irena Johnson about to have her collar felt during the tour-bus war

SHAKESPEARE'S CHILDREN

Archie Davis senior, Mrs Mathews and Bill Fisher, All Justin's Avenue, enjoying a wedding reception at the Tyler Street Boy's Club

The Brook children. Colin, on the right, shot me with his catapult!

Honoured and proud to have a drink with 'Desert Rat' Bill 'Spodger' Sparrow of Justin's Avenue

DANNY KEANEY WITH DALE LE VACK

My old mate 'Fluff' Jones, aged 8. I couldn't find a photograph of 'Fluff' so I had a drawing done from memory

SHAKESPEARE'S CHILDREN

Paradise: On the farm in Norfolk in the 1950's

A Norfolk soil bucket

DANNY KEANEY WITH DALE LE VACK

David and Terry Smith with Sister Ann in their summer gear

Paradise: On the farm in Norfolk in the 1950's

With Seamus O'Rourke at the Keaney family residence in County Leitrim.

Chapter Six
A BATTLE OF WILLS IN STRATFORD

I think we all have defining moments and looking back I'd say one of mine came when I returned to Warwickshire. It was the summer of 1964 and a big year for Stratford because it celebrated the 400th anniversary of the birth of William Shakespeare. Not that I knew or cared at the time.

I had grown into a big bloke, well over six feet tall and with huge hands like Fafa. The days were gone when I was a wimp, inclined to back away from confrontation. I had been on the wrong end of too many beatings and I had decided that life was too short to allow anyone to slap me about any more.

I was prepared now to stand up for myself, but did not intend to go looking for trouble. I'd hoped that all the gratuitous violence of my childhood and adolescence in Stratford had ended when people became adult and looked for other things in life.

I was wrong. Trouble soon came looking for me. In the first few days I walked down the town looking for old chums from Justin's Avenue and was at the old bus station at the bottom of Bridge Street when I came across a trouble-maker I didn't know. It was Tommy from Quinton, known as a hard man with a short temper. He was wearing motorbike leathers, had long greasy hair and an ugly face. This young man obviously fancied himself as a typical "Rocker".

I paid no attention to Tommy, but from the "hard" stares I was getting it was clear he had a problem with me. Tommy and the gang of his motorbike pals decided they recognised me as someone who'd been causing them aggravation at the Peyton Street community centre. I'd never been there.

The next thing I got a smack in the mouth when I wasn't expecting it, which loosened some teeth and split open my lips. I decided not to fight Tommy's gang that day and walked off seething, determined to find out who they were. I was given his name and told he was down at the bus station most evenings.

I took a couple of friends down there the next day and found "hard man" Tommy and his cronies loafing about in their habitual corner. He was talking to his mates, so I tapped him on the shoulder. As soon as he turned round, I let him have one straight in the mouth.

He went down on the floor with his mouth all cut open and didn't get up. None of his mates wanted to tangle with mine, so we walked off and had a few beers to celebrate.

The fall of "Greaser Tom" must have been talked about in town, because a week or two later I was sitting alone at the bar early one evening in the Anchor (now the Encore) at the bottom of Bridge Street, hoping to see pals I hadn't met since arriving from Norfolk, and renew a friendship or two. Instead Mick Simms, another greaser, who years before had thrown a house brick at me when I was on the ground, walked into the bar with some of his chums.

Mick fancied himself as a hard man and didn't think he would have any trouble with Danny Keaney, who always backed off fights when he could. One of his motorbike mates had had an accident and was on crutches. Mick grabbed it and hit me over the head with the crutch as hard as he could.

"Back in Stratford again, Keaney?" he said, with a sneer on his face.

"Bollocks," I thought.

"Simms, you are going to have to have it."

But not that night…I'd get even with Mick Simms when I had a few mates with me.

The next evening I went into the Anchor with a group of friends including Fluff Jones, Colin Brook and Rupert Sharlot. Mick was there, sitting at the bar again with a group of his cronies.

"Right, me and you from last night," I said.

He laughed because he thought I'd be no trouble, so I wiped the smile off his face with a good right hook. Down he went, but not for long, and the fight started in earnest. It was one of Stratford's epic fights and witnessed by dozens of people….a real battle.

The punch-up started in the pub, went through it onto the pavement outside, carried on in the middle of the road in Waterside, and eventually moved onto the pavement opposite, where it ended. The punches were flying like it was some Western movie and the growing crowd was thoroughly enjoying it. The noise and the shouting attracted an even larger crowd, including shocked theatre goers, many of them foreigners; their notion of genteel Stratford smashed to pieces. There was never any sign of the police.

The fight was a battle of will power and strength. We were both covered in blood and soon reached a stage of exhaustion, but I was the fitter and stronger. Mick was determined not to lose face by coming second best to someone he regarded as a "softie" with no reputation as a fighter. I was not prepared to be on the receiving end of anything from anyone any more. I knew I would never again back down in the face of provocation. The worm had turned.

"Take that you bastard, and this is for the brick you smashed on my head!" I heard myself saying as I kicked him in the groin as he lay gasping for breath.

In the end, I had beaten the shit out of him and given him no mercy even when he was on the ground. There was no enjoyment in doing it, but Mick needed to be taught a lesson and I was not prepared to face intimidation from him for the rest of our teenage years. It worked, and after that he became a fairly good mate and now in later life is regarded as an excellent bloke. We all change as we get older.

In 1964 youngsters had a limited choice in what to do at night but the pick of the town was the disco at the Drake Rooms above the Plymouth Arms in Wood Street, the *Cross Keys*, the Queen's Head in Ely Street, and the old Red Lion in Bridge Street. There were many more pubs in Stratford at that time than there are now.

The night-spot at the *Plymouth Arms* was a well known haunt and popular with youngsters from as far as Coventry and Redditch. Rivalry between different gangs from different towns soon developed, and we small-town Stratfordians discovered how some of the Coventry lads meant business, and could even be dangerous if provoked.

Fluff and I got involved in a series of arguments on successive Friday nights with some Coventry boys and although there was no punch-up on these nights it was building up towards a big one and they started to make threats which went beyond the realm of larking about.

"Next week we're bringing guns and we'll fucking shoot you bastards," they warned Fluff and me.

We thought they were joking but the following Friday we heard from our mates that they had indeed turned up with a firearm. We "scarpered" not wanting to call their bluff and laid low for the night. In their frustration at not being able to find us, they fired a shot from a car outside the *Plymouth Arms*.

Del Paddock, a mate of ours, was sitting on his motorbike innocently watching some "carry on" over the road outside the club when he was hit by pellets from the shotgun. They pulled up beside him in the car, wound down the window, and fired at poor old Del, who took the blast in the legs. He limped for the rest of his life, but what upset him most that night was that the brand new front tyre on his bike had been punctured.

The town was soon crawling with coppers from all over Warwickshire and it was on the local TV news the following evening, but Fluff and I kept well out of the way. I do not want to give the impression that the Plymouth Arms was a bad place full of thugs. It was policed strictly by one of the toughest men in the town. Ron Millward, a friend of our family, was the chief bouncer and didn't take any lip from anyone. He had a short fuse.

He was playing rugby for Coventry at that time where he had a reputation for being a dirty player, even at that level. Ron was one of those bouncers who were hard but fair. He'd tell you once, tell you twice and then he'd clout you. If you gave him respect he wouldn't duff you – but if you crossed him you were in for trouble because he would punch you hard, especially youngsters like me who were inclined sometimes to get out of hand.

He clouted me two or three times for various misdemeanours and I ended up each time with a swollen head like a football. There was Ron, Ray Knight and my brother-in-law Ted Dovey, married to my sister Kathleen, who later was killed in a car crash along with his son.

Ted and I fell out one night and they all kicked the shit out of me. I went down the concrete steps and my face was a terrible mess. Of course, I deserved it – it was all part of growing up, the male hormones kicking in on a Friday night. Years later, Ron decided that I was so good at taking a punch that he invited me to play rugby for Stratford.

Occasionally, if things got out of hand after a "ruck" at the *Plymouth Arms*, or some other pub, we'd end up in the cells at Stratford Police station. It tended to be me, Fluff and "Spud" Murphy.

"Oh fuck me, not you lot again," P.C. Mick Mole would say and drag us off to the police station for a night in the cells. A copper would go down to the Cozy Corner Café and get us breakfast in the morning. I didn't mind that at all because I didn't get any breakfast at home, but eating egg and bacon with a spoon proved a bit tricky. In those days we didn't get charged with anything because they understood it was just youthful high spirits – they just wanted us off the streets for the night.

One night we were left in the charge of a young cadet and "Fluff" got him to take him to the toilet for a pee. "Spud" found the key to the cell and somehow he ended up locking the youngster in it with the three of us on the outside. The cadet was terrified his sergeant would come back and find him locked up. We thought it was a great joke at the time, but the young copper was in tears, so we let him out.

"See you next week lads," the Sergeant would say as he let out on the Saturday morning.

"Was the breakfast to your liking?"

"Bit more butter on the toast next week and can you tell the cook to give us poached eggs with runny yolks?"

"Will do lads," he would say as he waved us off. Those were the days, but not all of them were as genial as him - as I found out to my cost.

It was New Year's Morning, well after midnight, and we were in our late teens and hanging around town having drunk too much - and generally behaving like arseholes - but not actually breaking the law. I think the mob included Fluff, Spud, Sammy Windsor and one or two others whose names I can't remember.

There was a ladies fashion shop at the time in one of the streets in the town centre and a group of lads we did not know, but were also drunk, decided the mannequins in the front window had to come out on the pavement. We were around when they smashed the glass, pulled out the mannequins and decided to put on the bras, skirts and dresses which they thought was a real hoot. We thought it was a right lark too, but weren't part of it.

After a few minutes we heard the sirens - and the lads dressed as women scarpered. We didn't run for it because we hadn't done anything. The police cars rolled up and the coppers inside leapt out and soon took an entirely different view. Despite our protests, we were arrested and hauled off to the police station. In fact, although we were supposed to be the bad lads in town, we didn't do vandalism – one of the few things we weren't into.

We had either done it, or knew who'd done it - according to this big ugly Duty Sergeant from Leamington, who sneered at our vehement denials. Then he started to get cross and began threatening me because he said I was lippy. Next thing he lost it completely. I could not believe it when he started hitting hard me across the chops.

"It was you Danny wasn't it?"

"No it fucking wasn't!"

Clump, another fist in the face came my way.

He knocked me off my chair at least half a dozen times.

"Come on you little bastard Danny, you'll tell me who those yobs are who did it if it wasn't you - or I can go on doing this all night," he snarled with his nose pressed against my face.

Clump again.

It hurt a lot and my nose was bleeding. I was completely gobsmacked because I had not been back from Norfolk for long, where that kind of thing just did not happen.

"It wasn't us, you tosser!" I exclaimed again.

Every time I said no, I got hit again. I think the others had some as well but they were in a different room. He went on clobbering me and I really began to wonder if I wouldn't end up in hospital. It ended as suddenly as it began when one of the duty coppers came into the station off his beat.

"Christ, I've seen it all now," he laughed. "There's a group of yobs in town dressed in bloody mini-skirts, bras and blouses. I thought I'd let you know in case it's got anything to do with that shop window being smashed."

They did collar the guilty lads, who confirmed they didn't know us when they were dragged down to the police station - and so we were released without apologies. As far as the cops were concerned we shouldn't have been there. We never complained – you didn't bother in those days.

One of the few things Jack Keaney ever did for me was to give me a job at Lumley Saville when I came back from Norfolk in 1964. I think he may have regretted it shortly afterwards and in fact while I worked for him he fired me on six occasions until I left the company in 1967.

Once he sacked me for laziness, another time because I had long hair, a further time for throwing a lump hammer at him – and another time because I made a home-made cannon in the workshop with another bloke for a lark. We used a tube, welded the end and forced in oxy-acetylene gas as the explosive through a hole.

When we lit it, the projectile, a lump of wood, went by accident straight through Jack's office window and out the other window missing him narrowly while he was sitting at his desk.

It was unfortunate actually, because the cannon was not even pointing at the office when it went off, but somehow deviated from its course during its flight to find Jack's office. Three terrified men, including Jack, ran out of the office.

"What the fock's going on?" he shouted. He dismissed both of us on the spot and I trudged home. We were reinstated a few days later.

I remember the second sacking clearly too. One cold winter morning he came out of his office to find me.

"Danny, can you drive a bulldozer?"

"No."

"Well you are tomorrow morning."

There was a farm just outside Stratford and the farmer wanted a big hole in his yard filled up. It had been a pond at one time. Jack had arranged for trucks to come loaded with soil and tip this up next to the hole. The bulldozer would then fill it in and level it off.

"There'll only be one an hour Danny, so don't try to rush it, you'll have plenty of time," Jack reassured me.

When I arrived with the bulldozer there was a queue of trucks waiting to tip their soil in the yard. It had been raining and snowing and I didn't know what I was doing. I got the bulldozer stuck deep in the mud in the middle of the pond and realised to my horror it would have to be pulled out. Lumley Saville had to bring in another bulldozer on the back of a low-loader to get the job done, and I was instructed to go back the next morning with brother Cavan to dig out the first machine and clean up the tracks and the engine.

Overnight it froze so we decided to put some diesel on the ground to set fire to it to thaw it out. It didn't work so we brought in bales of straw, scattered the bales around the bulldozer, soaked the straw with more diesel and set fire to it. It went up with a thump as we set it alight and was soon out of control. The bulldozer was burnt out.

I got a bollocking but the job needed finishing so they brought in another bulldozer and more trucks were organised to bring in soil. I waited and waited in the cold, trying to keep myself warm. It was snowing and the temperature was below freezing and I was really fed up.

I tried to find some shelter in a shed used to house calves. Each one had a separate partition heated with a lamp. I sat in with one of the calves and was soon asleep. The farmer found me, phoned Jack, and I woke up to find them both looking at me over the door snuggled up with the calf in the warmth of the lamp.

"What the fock do you think you're doing?" the Irishman asked angrily. I was allowed to finish the job, but one day the bulldozer's blade caught the supporting pillar of an ancient barn, demolishing the pillar and causing the barn to partially collapse---more big trouble.

I really was accident prone because one week after the farm incidents I was told by Jack to drive a three ton flat bed lorry to Blackburn with a cargo of replacement tracks for a bulldozer on hire in the area.

"How much driving have you done Jimmy (his nickname for me)?" He asked ,knowing full well what the answer was.

Jack knew and didn't care that I had never driven a lorry before, or that I had only passed my driving test a couple of weeks before. I loaded up and headed for the town centre where I ran over a bicycle propped up on the corner of Greenhill street. I then demolished a set of traffic lights in Manchester by dragging the side of the lorry along the supporting pillar—the local constabulary weren't pleased and held me up for two hours making accident reports--- much worse was to come.

Making up for lost time I was going far too fast on the Cliviger Road, Blackburn, when I failed to spot the mini-van in front was parked and I hit it an almighty blow, sending it forward at a fair rate of knots and compacting it into two thirds of its original length.

The door of the van opened and through the steam from the lorry's shattered radiator I saw this poor man spill onto the road clutching his head and heading in my direction. He accused me of being mad because I was laughing---it was quite funny. The police eventually arrived and wanted an explanation---as they do. I told the policemen that the van was rolling backwards down the hill and it had taken me by surprise. This was a story I made up on the spur of the moment. The angry van driver then took a swing at me and was jumped on by two police officers and told to calm down. I finally got to the job two days later --- never did like rushing.

I was not the only one in our gang prone to having car accidents. Fluff Jones had bought his first car, a sit-up-and-beg Ford Popular. He'd left it parked down the Warwick Road in the drive of his girl-friend's house with whom he'd broken up and didn't want to be seen retrieving it. So in the dead of the night we drove Ian (Cilla) Clark's car to within a hundred yards of the drive. Fluff and I took a towing rope and crept up to the house – attaching the rope to the front of the Ford Popular and the other end to the back of Ian's car. We got it out onto the road but it wouldn't start and to add to the problem it didn't have any lights. I ran back to Ian's car so he'd know when Fluff was at the wheel. The long rope was strong enough to pull the Ford without the engine running.

We drove towards Fluff's house without lights and all went well until a car started to overtake – completely unaware of the towing rope. It just managed to get past without an accident although it did hit the rope. A narrow escape but we got it back without further mishap. The next day – it had been snowing and the roads were iced up - we decided to go to Alcester for a few drinks, got it started and arrived in Alcester. There was Fluff, me, Mick McLoughlan and "Spud" Murphy in the group. On the way home the car stalled at the top of Redhill so we decided to push it down the long slope on the A46 towards Stratford.

"I'll drive, I know how to start a car," volunteered Mick, who did not bother to tell us he didn't have a clue how to actually drive a car. We got the engine started and it began to career faster and faster, swaying violently from side to side when it hit top speed.

"For fuck's sake Mick - what are you doing?" I shouted as the car, by now out of control and on the wrong side of the road, headed straight towards a high-sided fully- loaded coal lorry. With seconds before a head-on collision I grabbed the steering wheel and wrenched it out of his hand. The car lurched to the left and there was an almighty bang - followed by silence. We were now airborne and hit the ground rolling, taking out at least 40 yards of hedge

We came to a halt with Spud screaming.

"I've got glass in my eyes," he cried. After that we realised how lucky we'd been to survive it and climbed out gingerly. Fluff was in a state of shock and had to go to hospital. The police arrived and luckily it was our favourite Stratford policeman PC Mick Mole.

"Christ, not you buggers again," he shouted when he saw who the passengers were. The police never found out Fluff wasn't driving so we got away with it. I think it was the nearest any of us came to meeting our maker.

After three years working for Jack, in which time I was frequently bored, I joined Dick Kingston at R J Kingston Engineering, steel fabricators, now in Timothy Bridge Road. Dick had originally worked at Lumley Saville under my father and branched out on his own.

Dick and I seemed to get on well and I knew that if I got out of line he'd stick one on me. If he wanted me to do overtime he'd lock all the doors and put the Alsatian in the workshop with me. I learned my main skills working for Dick and respected him. Deep down, however, my heart has always lain in farming and every job outside that sector I've hated. Perhaps that's why in the end I was unemployable, which is why for most of my working life I've been self-employed.

Jack, who had sacked me so many times, never regretted my being signed up by Dick and he continued to work at Lumley Savile until he retired. He had heart and kidney problems and spent some time before he died in hospital, 18 months before Mabel died of heart trouble.

The girls, Cavan and I wanted to give the old boy a good send off and there was a family service at St Gregory's Church before he was buried in the cemetery. A lot of Jack's work friends and his brothers and sisters turned up as well. I suppose that looking back he really did have a wicked sense of humour that perhaps I did not appreciate during my childhood and youth.

So Jack would have been amused the night before the funeral when I took the Norfolk contingent for a few drinks to the Squirrel which had recently opened. The landlord tolerated the Norfolk rural accents for much of the evening but began to get sarcastic about my relations to the point I found it offensive and decided he had to have it.

I lunged at him across the bar and dragged him across the top and then I put in a Keaney hay-maker. Trouble was it missed the landlord completely and thwacked my brother-in-law Harvey in the eye. He had a corker the next morning for the service but found it all highly amusing.

I got banned from the pub, of course, but took no notice and drank there whenever I felt like it. The landlord was bloody ignorant and nearly got what was coming to him. I still regret not hitting the bastard, even though I'm much more tolerant these days.

Introduced to the Oval ball...

I had played a little rugby at secondary school in Norfolk but was not really interested in it at that stage. When I came to Stratford I found I knew a lot of blokes who were playing club rugby at various levels and gradually drifted into it. John Marshall, Brian Young and Peter Jackson had started a club at Shipston and at the start of the 1969 season they persuaded me to go along and play a game for them. I enjoyed it and joined the club.

Gradually, I found I was not a bad player. I had no great speed or ball skills, but enjoyed being in the engine room, getting stuck in, tackling, rucking and mauling. I found my strong arms and upper body strength, from the farming years, stood me in good stead.

I became an aggressive player, but prepared to retaliate initially only if someone kicked me on the ground or swung a punch at me. Later on, when playing for Stratford, I was prepared to initiate the "retaliation" because in those days you always tried it on with your opposite number – and in my case as a flanker the half-backs - to establish your presence on the field.

You'd let them know you were there if you could get your hands on them, hoping to intimidate. Sometimes you would come off worse against a grizzled old forward, but at that level we had to go for it because we played the top junior clubs in the Midlands the North and Wales.

Mind you, it wasn't at Stratford that I received my worst hammering. That came in a Shipston game against the small village club Claverdon, one of the rival clubs, who played at Ossetts Hole Lane on Yarningale Common. It was an ill-tempered match with quite a few players on both sides "mixing it".

I suppose I was one of the ringleaders on our side, being my usual aggressive and obnoxious self on the rugby field. It all came so naturally to me because I was enjoying it so much.

Suddenly, off the ball, when I wasn't expecting it, this big guy – I've always suspected he was a "ringer" and not one of their regular players because he was too good – dished out a really big one in the mouth and down I went. All I remembered were stars in my eyes as I lay there.

They picked me up and rushed me to Warwick hospital where I ended up with a loose tooth, thirteen stitches on my lips and inside my mouth. I remember looking in the mirror and the only thing I could see was what seemed to be white fat bulging out of the inside of my gob. The nurse confirmed it was fat.

"Bugger me, my lips are going to be like this forever," I said to myself in the mirror. In fact, it's a part of the anatomy that heals quickly and a few weeks later no one would have known I'd been clobbered on the mouth by the wicked Claverdon forward. That '' wicked Claverdon forward'' I have since found out was a gentleman named Peter Braithwaite who was once a schools heavyweight boxing champion and a founder member of Claverdon Rugby club.

At the end of the season I was talking to Ron Millward, who was by now playing for Stratford and coming towards the end of his career. He remembered me from years before at the *Plymouth Arms* and that I could take a punch.

"Why don't you come and play for Stratford?" he asked.

I joined for the start of the 1973 season. The club had a strong fixture list in those days and it would not be an exaggeration to say that I felt extremely overawed when I turned up to play in my debut match for the 1st XV. I was hoping my ability to knock people over, retrieve the ball in the loose, and get in amongst it using my upper body strength and huge hands, would stand me in good stead.

It was against Cambridge City RFC and Ron was playing. Soon after the whistle went, Ron came up to me and gave me an instruction about dealing with their six feet eight inch second row forward, who was also the opposition's top lineout jumper.

"He's as soft as shit. When they call a short lineout, I want you to go in opposite. Don't attempt to catch the ball because you won't - just punch him. Don't worry Danny he won't dare chin you if he knows I'm behind you. So you just punch him to stop him getting the ball."

It was Ron's idea of a set-up to introduce me to 1st XV rugby. The guy was certainly not as soft as shit and when I punched him there was a bellow of rage like a wounded bear. He thumped me on the top of the head with a mighty blow that gave me a headache for a week. Ron just let me take it and made no attempt to intervene.

I only ever scored one try for Stratford in my 1st team career and the player who made it for me always swore afterwards he wouldn't have chipped the ball forward, for me to catch it on the line and dive over, if he'd known it was me he was trusting to do the job.

Frank Russell was our star fly-half who had played first-class rugby in South Africa and he always avoided passing me the ball, even if I was next in the line – in fact, it was a standing joke between us. Frank always believed I had a crap pair of hands but a bloody good pair of feet for kicking opposing players.

"You aren't worth passing to," he'd tell me. I think I could have waited till judgement day for a pass from Frank.

I'll never forget the day he made the exception to the Russell rule and chipped the ball neatly through their backs towards the line. He didn't know it was me and must have thought I'd appeared from nowhere - and he was astonished I didn't fumble it. It was the very first game of our centenary season and it was against Banbury. So I scored the first try for the 1st XV in the 100th year. Mind you, I never got another pass from Frank --- don't blame him.

I gradually got a reputation at Stratford as a wild and aggressive player and had to be ordered to calm down on many occasions by the skipper. Too often the warnings were ignored and I got sent off, or gave away yet another penalty. However, the selectors must have thought I was worth having in the side. In those days every team at that level needed two or three players who knew how to dish it out.

Another "basher" in our side was Fluff Jones, who made his debut for Stratford 1st XV in the second-row, shortly after I had made mine as a flanker. A former Shipston player like me, he was very tough on the field, certainly someone you'd want on your side, but it would have helped if he could have seen what was going on - as soon as he took off his milk bottle lens glasses, he could see nothing for about 10 minutes.

One day he kicked a bloke on the floor and gave him a real good booting. The referee blew his whistle and all hell was about to be let loose. Whenever Fluff was caught kicking someone on the ground, he had a ready-made excuse that what he was doing was legal.

"I'm wearing football boots ref, they've got plastic studs. They wouldn't hurt a fly," he reassured the referee, who let him off. If it had been me, I'd have been sent off.

He got in a fight at Keresley RFC and both he and the other player were sent off. When they left the field they were still fighting. They reached the changing room, still fighting, and the other bloke pulled a knife on Fluff. I'm not sure what happened next. Fluff did not continue playing the game for long, after I stopped. I think he missed me, especially the nights out after the game.

Perhaps the most controversial punch I ever dished out was on Roger Bacon, one of the Stratford centres and a public school type. He had played previously for one of the toffee-nosed London clubs including Rosslyn Park and Richmond, and was a strong-running player with an excellent pair of hands. The trouble was he fancied himself too much.

We were playing Stoke-on-Trent, a very strong club, which that day fielded thirteen county players, plus an England Under-23 winger, so we had our work cut out. We went out there fired up, but as often happened, I got too fired up and lost it. Half way through the first half, the skipper came up and put his arm around my shoulder.

"Danny, for Christ's sake calm down."

I didn't know what I'd done and twenty minutes later the skipper came up again.

"For fuck's sake Danny calm down, or we'll lose you for the rest of the game because you'll get sent off."

It was one of those red mist days for me and in the second half I had a vague recollection of punching a player in the balls as he ran past me in the opposite direction. I thought it was a Stoke player who had been getting cheeky with me. I didn't find out what I'd done until we were in the changing rooms afterwards. Roger Bacon was apoplectic and shouting at the top of his voice. It seems that he was the one I'd punched in the balls during the second-half.

"If Danny Keaney ever plays for Stratford Rugby Club again, I'm leaving. I've played for some of England's top clubs and I've never met a bloody maniac like him before," he complained at the top of his voice.

I thought I had really buggered things up for myself and would get sacked from the club. Fortunately for me, Malcolm Greenslade, the skipper, thought otherwise.

"Suit yourself Roger if you want to leave Stratford, we won't have any prima donnas in this club," he told him. Roger Bacon did go on playing but our relationship was never warm after that.

I came up against Stoke's England Under-23 wing on another occasion when he was playing for Moseley United and made it my business to avenge previous humiliations, in which he had made me feel like an old farm carthorse when he side-stepped me effortlessly, and accelerated away.

This time I was ready for him and lined him up from the right angle in time to get him before he could side-step, as on previous occasions. I was travelling very quickly (for me) and hit him just right.

Down he went on the ground and let go of the ball. The trouble was his knee hit me hard in the neck area. I was paralysed from the neck down and had never been so frightened in my life. I lay there helpless. There wasn't too much sympathy from anyone as they tried to revive me.

"Can you feel anything now?" someone asked putting a hand on my back.

"No I can't," I replied. Five minutes later someone asked the same question. I was sweating with fear, convinced I'd broken my neck, but they continued to cajole me and very slowly, very slowly, feeling returned first in the arms then down the body.

"Oh, he'll be OK soon," said the referee waving away the stretcher.

And so it was. I picked myself up painfully and continued to play the rest of the game. These days there would be ambulances, air ambulances, compulsory hospitalisation and no further rugby for weeks.

I think I was sent off about ten times while playing for Stratford. The reason I was sent off was because of my aggressive nature. It all went back to my childhood when people picked on me continually - and in my sub-conscious I wasn't going to have any shit from anyone.

It was stupid because sometimes I'd commit a serious offence right in front of the referee. Once I even pushed the referee out of the way to get at an opposing player.

We were playing Hereford, a very physical side, and as I came into a maul I noticed the head of one of their very ugly props was sticking out. I rammed my head straight into his face as I went in, to make it look like an accident. He had chinned me earlier in the game.

All hell broke loose for at least two minutes. The referee took ages to control the situation and called me and the Hereford captain over to him. He stood between us to keep us apart. The Hereford captain continued to threaten me loudly with what he and the others were going to do to me, which annoyed the referee.

"Look calm down, calm down, it was an accident. Pack it up or you're going to have to go!" The referee warned him several times but he continued to call me every name he could think of and so the tension increased.

"Fuck this, I've had enough of this twat," I thought.

So I pushed the referee out of the way and "twatted" him as hard as I could. It all started again. The upshot was that I had to walk, which was fair enough. I think the referee was a professor of psychology at Warwick University. I had conned him once but not twice.

I was rummaging through some old drawers in the garage at home and came across two reports from referees who had had occasion to send me off the field.

St Thomas Hospital v Stratford-upon-Avon RFC (1978)

Detailed Report of Incident

The Stratford player concerned deliberately went over the top of a ruck, stamping on several players of the opposition team. Earlier, I had cause to warn the Stratford-upon-Avon captain that his pack were using their feet to kick opponents illegally and that I would send off any offender I could see repeating this action. An incident had occurred at a previous ruck and although I could not pin down the offender, as I was unsighted, it was made clear to me that it was the Stratford number eight. This did not in fact influence my decision. I feel that if the allegations were correct this player is a danger to the game of rugby. Also, I must point out that a member of the Stratford Committee was most concerned at the incident and assured me his club would deal with him immediately.

Our man on the line was Dr. Ken Holley, a long-standing and much respected official at Stratford RFC. After the game I told him that I should not have been sent off by the referee who had not even seen the incident and was clearly influenced by what the opposition players had told him.

"Ah!" said Ken. "But you should have been sent off ten minutes before that."

Old Dixonians RFC v Stratford-upon-Avon RFC (1983)

Detailed Report of Incident

Line out awarded to Stratford, 10 metres from their own goal-line. A wedge was formed and a player from the opposition (Old Dixonians) was seen to be offside. As I was blowing my whistle for the offside offence, the player concerned was hit in the face by the Stratford number eight, who then took part in a melee with two other players from the opposition. I blew my whistle again and called the Stratford captain to fetch the offending player to me whereof I informed him I was sending him off for striking an opposition player.

Not long afterwards I got an indefinite ban for a sending off and I was stopped from playing. Two years later, after Dr. Ken Holley our Chairman at the time argued that an indefinite ban was not a life ban, the Warwickshire committee was approached by Stratford to reconsider my case at a special disciplinary appeal hearing. They agreed to let me continue playing rugby, but warned me that if I stepped out of line once I'd be finished and banned for life.

They were swayed in making their decision largely because of the intervention of our President Tony Bird, who made a special plea on my behalf. He was friendly with John Richardson, the President of the Warwickshire RFU. Birdie convinced them that I was full of remorse, aware I needed to control my attitude and behaviour on the pitch, and that I was now a completely reformed character.

"We need you back at Stratford, we want you back, you've got years of good rugby in you, so don't let yourself down – what's more don't let me down, because I've put my good name down on the line for you," said Tony Bird in the changing room before making my debut as a reinstated player.

Does a leopard change its spots? I think I lasted for six games. We were playing Luctonians at Stratford, who were a good side then and now. I soon got pissed off with the laxness of the referee. He seemed blind to the fact that the opposition were committing a fundamental foul that anyone entrusted with a whistle in his hand on a rugby field should understand.

He was allowing the opposition to come round the side of the scrum to interfere with our ball. They were doing it all the time, because they were being allowed to get away with it.

"If they come round offside again, fucking 'stick' one on them and knock 'em out the other side," I said to our forwards.

The Stratford pack paid no heed to my plea and the Luctonian forwards continued to infringe, without any intervention from the referee. No one wanted to do anything about their offside infringements and I began to see the red mist again.

We kicked off for the second half and I caught the ball. Our forwards bound in on each side behind me, but one of their forwards ran round the side of the scrum again and blatantly tried to wrestle the ball off me.

"Fuck off," I said as I hit him and he went flying out the back of our scrum. All hell broke loose and the referee gave me my marching orders. I was ordered to walk and I knew that was it.

I was for it. The sentence was inevitable under the rules of the game. I was finished at the age of 32.

There was a delay to the start of the subsequent disciplinary hearing at the Quadrant Rooms, a Gentleman's Club in the centre of Coventry. I was with Brian Wilson and we went to the bar to have a few drinks before it started.

By the time the hearing did get underway we were a bit pissed, but I didn't really give a shit because I knew I was going to get a life ban. However, the sudden sight of that stupid referee made my blood boil. I asked the committee to tell the referee to leave, because I did not want to be in the same room as him.

"No, we can't do that. He was the referee and we must hear what he has to say," they said.

"Well, if you don't tell him to leave the room I'll throw the bastard through the window," I warned. The panel thought better of it, could probably tell I'd had a drink or two, and told the referee to leave the room.

"Bollocks, I'll have the bastard anyway," I said to myself, as he got up to leave.

So I chased him through the door as he ran out into the snooker room. Then I chased him round and round the snooker tables, bodies flying everywhere, but he managed to get away. He drove off in panic from the car park, but we leapt into Brian's car and chased the sod round Coventry. I don't know whether it made any difference to my sentence. I was banned for life and afterwards the worst bollocking of all came from Tony Bird.

"You told me you'd never let me down. I moved mountains for you to get you back playing again. Not only that you went to the hearing drunk," he ranted.

"No I didn't. It was only when I got there," I pleaded.

The consequences of a life ban began to sink in when I realised what I was missing and I became resentful that this committee of men had the power to stop me from the playing the game I loved. I thought it was extremely unfair - and down to an absence of refereeing integrity. The offside law had been breached so many times by the opposition that it was unreasonable to expect the victims of it not to retaliate in some way.

I decided to ring John Richardson, soon to become President of the English Rugby Football Union, who was a solicitor. In retaliation I thought I would cause a bit of mayhem. He picked up the phone.

"Hello Danny, nice to hear from you, what are you doing with yourself now that you're not playing rugby?" he asked.

"Well, actually John I am still playing rugby," I replied untruthfully.

"You can't," he said, with a discernible trace of irritation replacing the affable greeting.

"Well hang on a minute, what can you do if I am? You can't do anything about it, because you've already banned me for life."

"You can't play rugby," he repeated sternly.

"What are you going to do about it?" I repeated.

"Well, we can ban the people you play with and ban the club that selects you," he replied harshly.

I laughed. "Within twenty miles of Stratford there are at least thirty rugby clubs and some of them never play Stratford. I'll just turn up, give a false name, and they are none the wiser. I know it's not the same as playing for Stratford but at least I'm getting a game of rugby," I said, by now enjoying the fact I was winding up John.

"You can't do it Danny, you must not do it," he said again, the warning now being shouted down the line.

"Sorry John, but you've left me no option but to do it. I should not have been banned for life for that offence, considering what happened in that game."

The conversation ended there, but as far as John Richardson was concerned matters could not be left to rest. He made himself very busy the following week talking to fellow committee members about me and coming up with a way to deal with my dastardly plans.

He contacted the club to ask for a photograph of me which he said he would send to every rugby club in Warwickshire, warning them about a rogue player, banned for life, called Danny Keaney and the consequences for their club of selecting me to play. I was not to be invited to play again under any circumstances. Stratford Rugby Club wrote back to say there were no photographs available of Danny Keaney.

The matter was left there, so no "wanted" picture of me ever appeared in Warwickshire club-houses, which was actually something of a disappointment not be immortalised by a "wanted" picture like Wyatt Earp or Billie the Kid.

Ironically, Peter Jackson, (famous England winger) the chairman of the Disciplinary Panel who banned me for life, was guest of honour at the Stratford RFC annual dinner in the early summer and was given the job of presenting the 'Clubman of the Year' Trophy to none other than Danny Keaney.

I found it very satisfying to see him with his arm outstretched for the handshake beaming broadly at me to hide his obvious embarrassment - and to hear him muttering through his teeth.

"Well done!"

I did play rugby twice after that – the second time when I was forty - but I'd have to kill you if I told you who it was for! I'd also like the Disciplinary Panel to know that I had an exemplary game, played it in the right spirit and never considered punching anyone. At the time of my ban they should have been paying more attention to training their referees rather than victimising players. I can't imagine what would have happened in that game if it had taken place in New Zealand or South Africa. The injustice of my life ban still rankles with me.

Sometimes we were a wild bunch off the field as well as on it – which I suppose doesn't make Stratford RFC different from any other club in Warwickshire. There are no saints only sinners.

I've kept a letter dated 1st May 1981 following a disciplinary hearing at the rugby club after a series of controversial incidents at the notorious Wildmoor night club (now a very respectable health and fitness spa) on the Alcester Road at which our club was holding a men's function.

Unfortunately, the bar was also open to members of the public who were not part of the rugby club, or the "culture" of the game. The lads drank far too much and behaviour got out of hand, maybe outrageous, even if behind it all was a spirit of pretty harmless fun and the letting down of hair.

The letter was signed by Tony Bird, President of the club at that time and a well respected figure.

Stratford-upon-Avon RFC Committee

Dear Mr Keaney,

The disciplinary committee explained to you the acute embarrassment caused by articles in the Press concerning the appalling behaviour on the night of the male dinner.

It also explained to you the embarrassment of the President and the senior committee members who attended the dinner when the Mayor and other guests were shouted down.

We are advising all members of the club that such behaviour will not be tolerated in the future. The committee, however, was pleased with your frankness and honesty concerning this matter.

We are taking no action in the circumstances. However, they do ask you to bear in mind that at social events, especially when they are held out of our own clubhouse - and members of the public are present - our member's behaviour should be correct.

Signed

President A P Bird

I was perhaps lucky not to be banned from the club, although I can't remember exactly doing what I was supposed to have done, At least one other member did get banned. It seems he somehow lost his clothes during the evening but remained at the bar shamelessly clutching a pint of beer. Whether the town's mayor saw this naked apparition and its appalling beer belly I do not know.

Some of the rugby club boys at the Wildmoor Night Club that evening in 1981 went on in later years to become eminent members of the town's community in local government - and will probably be deeply embarrassed to be reminded of the incident when they read this book – but really it was just high spirits off the field rather than on it.

Looking back, I thoroughly enjoyed my years as a playing and then non-playing member and then official of Stratford Rugby Club, where I made many of my best friends, enjoyed a lot of high jinks and where I am still often to be found on Saturday afternoons with guys like Frank Russell watching the 1st XV games with a pint in my hand.

Chapter Seven

A FAMOUS IRISH RELATIVE

We bleed that the nation may live.
I die that the nation may live
Damn your concessions England,
We want our country

Jack Keaney had always been a staunch Republican and made no secret of it, even after the Ulster 'troubles' started in the early 1970s and the British Army found itself targeted by the IRA. For my father, there was no question in his mind - the British should not be on Irish soil and he regarded Northern Ireland as occupied territory.

Indeed, when he was in Stratford as a manager working for Lumley Saville, he collected money regularly from the Irish who worked for him. This was sent back to Ireland to fund Republican causes.

I don't know whether this cash went to Sein Fein, or to the Provisional IRA to purchase arms - and I certainly did not ask him any questions about it. It was not until much later in life that I realised, and understood, the underlying cause of Jack's strong Republican views, which I never shared, but members of his generation in my family certainly did.

However, as I became older and made contact with my kinsmen in Ireland, I developed a growing affection for her people and the land of my ancestors. I'm proud to be of Irish descent and I sympathise with those who struck out against what amounted to colonial rule, although I suspect that much of the fighting and subsequent killing in the second half of the 20th century in Northern Ireland was avoidable.

Perhaps a peaceful settlement to the Ulster problem could have been achieved much earlier through democratic means if there had been no terrorism - with perhaps only a strong Civil Rights movement to lobby for change. 'Bloody Sunday', of course, for which the British Army was responsible, may have delayed a democratic political solution for more than 25 years. We only have the benefit of hindsight.

On the other hand, extreme sectarianism on both sides meant the respective leaders ignored the democratic process, which is surely why so many people died unnecessarily. Including my cousin Danny---murdered on his doorstep. One is always left asking the question....Why? Why? Why?

I have always considered it a paradox that some Republican-minded Irish people choose to emigrate here, to live under the protection of the Crown, enjoying the benefits of our Welfare State and National Health Service - while trying to undermine the State by giving succour to terrorism through funding it.

I do not criticise all Irish people for this anachronistic behaviour, for I lived among many "Paddies" during my childhood in Stratford and in the main have always found them warm, generous and good humoured people. Indeed, I think there is a strong Irish side to me, which those who know me cannot fail to recognise. My sisters always said I was too much like Jack to be able to get on with him.

Jack came from Glenfarne in County Leitrim, a border county, and was the son of Simon Keaney, who took his wife to America early in the 20th century.

Their four eldest children (Tommy, Jack, Paddy and Peggy) including my father were born in the USA. The Keaneys settled in Buffalo, New York State, not far from Niagra Falls, and eventually Simon did well enough to own one of the fire teams in Boston, which operated under contract to the insurance companies.

When Jack returned with his father and mother to Ireland, after the First World War and in the early days of the Republic, he was heavily influenced by the Cause because he was fed stories about his second cousin Sean McDermott (MacDiarmada).

Sean was one of the volunteers involved in the 1916 uprising in Dublin and a co-signatory of the Irish Proclamation, the conception of the Irish State. He was my third cousin and he was executed in 1916 for his part in the Rising.

A life-size statue by the Irish sculptor Albert Power was erected in Sean's memory and stands at the square in Kiltyclogher near where he was born. It is kept in immaculate condition and visitors can clearly see that one leg is shorter than the other.

This is because he suffered from Polio and was in poor health before he died. He always carried a cane and carried it with him into the General Post Office on Easter Monday, which the Irish Republicans occupied as their headquarters.

Secondly, there is a piece of cloth caught in his left hand on the statue. This signifies the blindfold which he had the option of wearing during his execution. He declined to wear the blindfold, stating he wanted to see those who were about to execute him. I have undertaken some research into the life of my kinsman and as a result I have now a vivid picture in my mind of the kind of man he was.

Historically, there has not been much recorded about the life of Sean McDermott, certainly less than the other co-signatories, and so I was intrigued to discover that Belfast author Gerard McAtasney had written a book about him. The book is titled *Sean MacDiarmada, the Mind of the Revolution* and it is available in most bookshops priced £15.

Thanks to Gerard's book I learned that Sean McDermott was born in late January 1883 in Kiltyclogher, County Leitrim, son of Donald, a carpenter and small tenant farmer, who was old enough to be his grandfather and had personal memories of the famine years in the 1840s. It is said that Donald built the pews in Glenfarne Chapel.

My father Jack's grandmother had a sister, Mary McMurragh, (McMorrow), who married Donald McDermott. Sean was the eighth of their 10 children. In fact, Sean's sister Bessie was godmother to Jack's younger sister Peggy, my auntie, and this is shown on her Baptismal Certificate issued by St Brigid's Church, Buffalo, in New York State in April 1915. So the Keaneys and McDermotts were close kinsmen.

The McDermott house, originally a thatched one-roomed cottage that was gradually extended into three rooms and five outhouses as the family became larger, was taken over by the Office of Public Works and now opens to the public during the summer months as a tourist attraction.

The house is in its original state, as far as possible, and was handed over to the State by Sean's brother Patrick. He was the final member of the family who sailed to America many years ago, and had no further use for the house.

It is just a few miles from Glenfarne, where the Keaneys lived, and Sean would have been told about how his mother's family at Glenfarne had suffered through eviction from the land they held as tenant farmers. Irish tenant farmers like my ancestors were victims of what was known as the rack-renting system, which enabled rich Anglo-Irish landlords to charge a very high rent - without themselves investing one penny in vital land improvements like drainage. The tenants were left to carry out the improvements as a result of their own industry and capital and if they did so their rent was increased in line with increased production.

Tenants were invariably charged the highest amount that could be paid for the land while enabling them to just about survive. Absentee landlords were nearly always notorious for refusing to make improvements to their land but their rents continued to rise through rack-renting, swallowing the lion's share of the farm's produce and the tenant's meagre living. It was a system that prevailed for hundreds of years and the peasantry in Ireland was regarded as the poorest and most down-trodden in Europe. So much for the fair play of the English!

The Most Rev. Dr Thomas Nulty, Roman Catholic Bishop of Meath, wrote: "The land of Ireland would at this moment still be in its original state of nature had it not been drained, cleared, reclaimed and fertilised by the enormous outlay of labour and capital which has been expended on it by the people of the present and their forefathers in past generations. The landlords contributed nothing, or next to nothing, for its improvement."

The unscrupulous landlord who evicted the McMorrow family was Captain Arthur Loftus Tottenham. He was known as 'Lofty', was a typical Anglo-Irish aristocrat of the Victorian era and thus a pillar of the local establishment. 'Lofty' was Liberal MP for Leitrim, and the family seat for hundreds of years was Glenfarne Hall, upon whose estate the McMorrow family, and indeed many of the Keaneys, were small tenant farmers.

The Tottenham family enjoyed vast wealth and spent much of their time in London. They were obviously not altruistic landlords, because they took a hard line with their poverty-stricken tenant farmers, rack-renting so they could support their own hedonistic lifestyle in what was for Ireland the desperate times of the second half of the 19th century.

'Lofty' was High Sheriff of Co Leitrim in 1886, as his father and grandfather had been before him, which meant his word was law to humble types like my ancestors - and there was certainly no appeal against eviction by such powerful landowners. The family were known collectively as the 'Glenfarne-Tudenham Tottenhams' and several generations served in the Rifle Brigade, including 'Lofty' himself.

I'm delighted to report that the house was burned down in "The Troubles" by vengeful local Republicans, like scores of other grand homes all over Ireland built by wealthy Anglo-Irish aristocrats. The property now belongs to the Forestry Commission and is known as Tottenham Forest. Ironically, the remains of my own ancestral home - a rather more modest structure - are to be found in the same forest, which I visited in 1999.

Despite the poverty and hardship, and sometimes hunger, Sean was a happy child in Corranmore, close to the village of Kiltyclogher, up to the age of nine, where he had a reputation for being a prankster with a love of mischief and a wild sense of humour. He enjoyed playing popular games such as *Hide and Seek*, *Fox and Geese*, *Bull in the Ring* and *Fool in the Middle*.

A visitor to the district wrote some time after Sean's childhood years: "I thought the donkey and the creils were only in existence on picture postcards but I found that it would be impossible to get along without them. There is only a little path to many of the houses on the side of a mountain so that only for his legs they could get nothing out or into the houses. They till none of the land except a little patch of potatoes and if this fails famine in the West is conspicuous in the papers. Hay and cattle are the principal source of income."

The fact much of the land went untilled was not, of course, because of idleness on the part of the local tenants, but because the landlord had failed to invest in making basic improvements to the land that could otherwise have sustained a diversity of crops. The famine was a direct result of that greed.

Life changed for the worse for Sean in 1892 when his mother Mary died, worn out through having so many children and the toil of a life spent in poverty. According to Sean's biographer Gerard MacAtasney, the loss was felt deeply by the lad, who was one of the younger children, and his grief was perhaps exacerbated by the fact his revered father was already 65.

In later life he confided in Kathleen Clarke, wife of the Republican leader Tom Clarke: "I have never known a mother's love and I have always longed for it. I have tried to picture what my mother would have been like. You fit that picture. When I see you with your children and the loving care you give them, I ache with the thought of never having known my mother. I missed all you give your children."

Sean was a good student at Corracloona National School, studying the core subjects of spelling, grammar, geography and agriculture, although he was hopeless at arithmetic, which was to cost him dear when he tried unsuccessfully to win a King's Scholarship to go to college to become a teacher. There was, however, a driving passion in Sean's mind from an early age for Irish history, which was to underwrite his future.

Among his most treasured possessions was R Barry O'Brien's *History of Ireland* published in 1897 when Sean was 14 and MacGeoghegan's *History of Ireland*, given to him as a present by his sister Katie some years later. These books, and others he had read earlier, showed how Ireland had suffered for hundreds of years under occupation by a foreign power.

In the midst of his studies as a young man, he was witness to events which were to influence still further his political instincts for Nationalism. In County Leitrim, as elsewhere in Ireland, the centenary of the 1798 Rebellion was commemorated with fervour, resulting in a reawakening of Irish Nationalist consciousness which had been in decline for some years towards the end of the 19th century and in the first years of the next.

Throughout 1898 rallies and commemorations were organised across Leitrim and neighbouring Sligo and 1798 Clubs formed in many localities. There was a very large Nationalist demonstration at Drumkeerin, which was 17 miles from Kiltyclogher, and it is hard to imagine Sean would have missed it, unless he was ill.

In the same year, agents of "Lofty's" unscrupulous heir carried out further high- profile evictions around Kiltyclogher which resulted in the destitution of 28 families – more than 100 people. Gerard MacAtasney writes that it was front page news in the *Sligo*

Champion - no doubt the talk of the local community - and likely to have excited further deep resentful feelings against the ruling Anglo-Irish class.

Sean's essays in preparation for his scholarship began to reveal study and knowledge of Irish history and the evil doings of the British ruling class. Whether this "extremist" viewpoint served to mark him down in the examinations will never be known. He may have revealed sympathies to the authorities that were judged too extreme for a teacher. In particular, it was clear that he admired Robert Emmet, leader of the revolution 100 years before.

Emmet, the son of a court physician, was an Irish nationalist, orator and rebel leader born in Dublin, took part in the 1798 Uprising and later led an abortive rebellion against British rule in 1803. He was captured, tried and executed for high treason. His family were wealthy Protestants who sympathised with the Catholics, believing they did not have fair representation in English Parliament. As an orator, some of Emmet's last words were made in a speech on the eve of his execution.

After the abortive 1798 uprising Emmet fled to France to avoid the many arrests that were taking place in Ireland. While he was in France Emmet garnered the support of Napoleon who promised to send troops and money when the upcoming revolution started. The Emperor did not keep his promise, however, and Emmet returned to Ireland without French help to prepare a new rebellion, with fellow revolutionaries Thomas Russell and James Hope.

Failing to seize Dublin Castle, which was lightly defended, the Rising in 1803 amounted to not much more than a violent riot, but on a large scale, and Emmet personally witnessed a dragoon being pulled from his horse and piked to death, the sight of which prompted him to call off the Rising to avoid further bloodshed. However, he had by then lost all control of his followers and in one incident the hated Lord Chief Justice of Ireland, Lord Kilwarden, was dragged from his carriage and hacked to death. Emmet became a martyr to the Cause in the 19th century and even two centuries later is revered throughout the land, especially by Romantics.

There is no doubt the seeds of activism had been sown in Sean's mind, but having failed the scholarship examinations he left Ireland for a short period and went to live in Glasgow, where he worked for an uncle who was a gardener. Gardening or labouring work did not appeal to the young man, so a few months later he returned to Ireland in July1904 at the age of 21 and enrolled in night school at Tullinamoyle near Dowra, County Cavan to study Irish and book-keeping.

Sean's teacher Patrick McGauran was not much older than himself. He had a deep love of everything pertaining to Irish history and literature, which he passed on to his student. He was, of course, a Nationalist himself, and his beliefs were imprinted on those who studied under him. One student wrote later "McGauran made rebels of us all!"

McGauran wrote of Sean: "Books relating to Ireland and her language, her heroes, or her history, were welcome to him, and he read with avidity all of them that he could lay his hands on. He also read poetry, especially Irish patriotic poetry and the poetry of Burns. Many a time at dances and gatherings he recited Emmet's Speech from the Dock and Father Mullin's poem *The Celtic Tongue*."

Gerard MacAtasney writes in the biography: "Having failed to attain his goal of the teaching profession and discovering manual labour was not to his liking, MacDiarmada had to make a decision regarding his future. By the time he left the Tullinamoyle Night School in the spring of 1905 he was 22 years of age and needed to obtain employment.

"Since there were no opportunities available around Kiltyclogher, he decided to follow his brother Daniel to Belfast in the hope of establishing a career. This move was to transform his life and see him catapulted into the maelstrom of Irish political activity."

He became a tram driver in Belfast and for several months he was highly successful, gaining early promotion, until he was caught by an inspector smoking on the platform of a tram while it was travelling with passengers aboard. Sean was unrepentant about his so-called misdemeanour and so given the sack. It was at this time he became a full-time Republican organiser and was paid a small allowance for doing so.

I think what makes me proudest to be a kinsman of Sean McDermott is that he believed strongly in a non-sectarian free Ireland, where Roman Catholics and Protestants would stand side by side against British rule - and following its defeat share in the government of a new free Republic.

After 1905, while living and working in Belfast for the Dungannon Clubs and the Irish Republican Brotherhood, he did his utmost to rid the city, and the countryside, of the ongoing hostility and historic animosity and hatred between the two creeds - and mould Irishmen in a spirit of nationhood together.

One of his closest colleagues Patrick McCarton, founder of the Dungannon Clubs, which were a springboard for the later formation of Sein Fein, wrote that the position of many Irish Protestants was "not actuated by a love of England but a hatred of the priest in politics."

Totally opposed to this non-sectarian philosophy was the Ancient Order of Hibernians, which fully supported the Irish Parliamentary Party, whose MPs under John Redmond served in the House of Commons in Westminster and were the successors of Robert Parnell.

Members of the Ancient Order of Hibernians had to be Roman Catholic and Irish born, or of Irish descent. An anti-English and anti-Protestant sentiment prevailed in its ranks into the 20th century, by which time it had developed into a militant lay-Catholic mass movement.

It was strongly opposed to secular ideologies such as those of the Irish Republican Brotherhood and tried to suppress the re-emergence of what it saw as a dangerous and upstart rival nationalist society. To its disgust, the IRB was non-sectarian and Protestants were among the senior figures in its ranks.

As a vehicle for Irish nationalism, the AOH greatly influenced the sectarian aspect of Irish politics in the early twentieth century. By 1914 this had saturated the entire island, fuelled not so much by sectarianism as by its utility as a patronage, brokerage and recreational association supporting Irish parliamentarians at Westminster.

After the 1916 Easter Rising the AOH melted away outside Ulster and its members were absorbed into Sinn Féin and the Irish Republican Army. In Northern Ireland in the 21st century, the AOH remains a visible but rather marginal part of the Catholic community.

Around the turn of the 20th century the people of County Leitrim were strong supporters of both the Irish Parliamentary Party, which had been able to secure some land reform, and the AOB, of which Sean was also a member at an early stage of his political career in Belfast. He soon moved away from their position when he realised there were many Protestants fighting for the cause of a Free Ireland.

Part of his job was to persuade members of the AOB in both Belfast and his home county to join the Dungannon Clubs and IRB. As a speaker at organised rallies he was frequently attacked and beaten up by the violent elements within the Hibernians who were determined that Sean and his fellow public speakers should be silenced.

Sean, who had been regarded as rather a naive country boy in 1905, soon developed rapidly under the tutelage of Bulmer Hobson, a young Quaker from Lisburn, and Denis McCullough whose family had been Republicans for several generations.

Both young men had become disillusioned with the moribund state of Irish nationalism in the early years of the 20th century, particularly in Belfast, and along with other young firebrands had decided to reorganise it away from the collection of drinking clubs it had become into a serious political organisation with the eventual aim of revolution. The result was the Dungannon Clubs and they began to spring up all over the country and in Scotland.

In 1908 Sean moved to Dublin, where he was rapidly promoted to the Supreme Council of the IRB and eventually became its elected secretary. He had become an important figure in several other republican organisations including Sinn Féin and the Gaelic League. He forged a reputation for himself as a good tireless organiser and a fine orator. In fact he became a popular and respected figurehead all over Ireland who could perform passionately, but sometimes with humour, in front of large crowds.

His speech at the Sinn Fein annual convention in Dublin made a deep impression and he was described as "striking handsome, and earnest, speaking with natural eloquence and with sincerity, which held his audience, gay and light-hearted with a gift of telling a humorous story and a tongue that was witty without being malicious."

In 1910 Sean became manager of the radical newspaper *Irish Freedom*, which he founded along with Bulmer Hobson and Denis McCullough. He also became a national organiser for the IRB. It was during these years that he met and was taken under the wing of the veteran Fenian Tom Clarke, who had served many years in a British prison and was determined to foment armed rebellion and revolution in Ireland. The two became inseparable.

Shortly afterwards Sean was stricken with polio and it took him two years to recover, leaving him with a permanent disability. One leg was now shorter than the other and he needed the assistance of a walking stick. The previously tall and strongly built man with striking good looks had become a frail figure physically, a shadow of his former self. It did not inhibit his political activities and if anything drove him to work even harder.

In November 1913 Sean was one of the original members of the Irish Volunteers, and he continued to work to bring that organisation under IRB control and move it away from those who sought to bring it under the control of the Irish Parliamentary

Party. Revolutionary hard-liners like Sean wanted the force to be used in the coming insurrection against British Rule and that is what happened with a breakaway movement.

In May 1915 he was arrested in Tuam, County Galway, under the Defence of the Realm Act, for giving a speech against enlisting into the British Army. It was around this time that he developed a relationship with Min Ryan who became the love of his life up to the time of his death.

She was born in 1884 and came from Tomcoole in County Wexford, where her family farmed 150 acres of land. This put Min in a higher social class than Sean and she attended the National University in Dublin as did nearly all of her 11 siblings, which was a remarkable academic achievement for one family. It is said she had first met Sean in 1904 while studying at the university.

Whether there was any romantic attachment however before 1915 remains a matter of speculation. It is doubtful. She went to France and Germany for two years and then lived in London where she formed a branch of Cumann na mBan, the female wing of The Irish Volunteers, before returning to Dublin in 1914. The first letter between them is dated March 1915 and its tone suggests the couple were very familiar with each other. His busy lifestyle meant he often had to let her down on pre-arranged dates but this fiery Republican woman expected him to put his work for the Cause before romance and she was always patient with him.

I am really sorry I cannot go out tonight. If I had heard from anyone early today – even before I left at two o'clock I could have kept the night free. Tomorrow night, which ought to be fee, I have a meeting at a very awkward hour, nine o'clock......

Following his release from prison in September 1915, he joined the secret Military Committee of the IRB, which was charged with the task of planning the Rising. Indeed Sean McDermott and Tom Clarke were the people most responsible for it.

The Keaney family concluded afterwards that Sean, who was nobody's fool, was well aware that militarily the 1916 Easter Uprising would probably fail - but its historic consequences would guarantee the eventual emergence of a free Irish nation. He was prepared to give his life, if necessary, for that and, with other leaders, become martyrs to freedom.

According to my sisters our great uncles and aunts and his kinsmen believed that Sean and the other leaders saw martyrdom as the only way to shake the nation out of its relative apathy towards the Cause in the years leading up to the First World War. Not all the leaders wanted to fight at that time however. Indeed, according to my research, Professor MacNeill, the nominal leader of the Irish Republican Brotherhood, had arranged for a parade to be held on Easter Sunday, but later found it was to be the base of the rising and he cancelled the event.

The cancellation went largely unheeded, for the parade was perceived by many Nationalists as the opening act of the Irish War for Independence. It took place instead the following day on Easter Monday, but had an unpromising start from a military point of view.

There was confusion caused by a rash of conflicting orders sent out to the Irish Volunteers – the main strike force - from their headquarters and the decision taken by the rebel leaders to postpone their action arranged for Easter Sunday 23rd April, until the next day.

Patrick Pearse and the Irish Volunteers, along with James Connolly and the socialist Irish Citizen Army, and the Cumann na mBan, the female wing of The Irish Volunteers, were with the leaders of the Uprising as they assembled at various pre-arranged meeting points in Dublin.

Before noon they set out to occupy a number of imposing buildings in the inner city area with a force of around one thousand armed men and women. Sean McDermott was with the other leaders who marched along Sackville Street, now O'Connell Street.

Once the GPO had been secured as the headquarters of the Irish soldiers, the British union flag was removed and two Irish flags were hoisted onto the roof of the GPO. Other outposts around Dublin were captured by the Irish soldiers at the same time as the Post Office.

These buildings were chosen because the Irish could command the main routes into the capital from them and also because of their strategic position in relation to the major military barracks. The occupied buildings included the Dublin Castle, the Four Courts, Jacob's Factory, Boland's Bakery, the South Dublin Union, St. Stephen's Green and later the College of Surgeons.

Early in the afternoon of Easter Monday Patrick Pearse read out the Proclamation of the Irish Republic to the Irish people. It had been written and printed at the headquarters of the Irish Citizen Army in Liberty Hall a few days before.

Irishmen and Irishwomen, in the name of God and of dead generations from which She receives her old tradition of nationhood, Ireland, through us, summons her children to her flag and strikes for her freedom...... We declare the right of the people of Ireland to the ownership of Ireland.

There was little fighting on the first day, since British intelligence had failed hopelessly. The properties targeted were occupied virtually without resistance and immediately the rebels set about making them defensible. The GPO was the nerve centre of the rebellion, serving as the headquarters and the seat of the provisional government which had been declared. Five leaders were based in the GPO including Sean McDermott.

The rebels waited in anticipation of a British military onslaught, forward posts looking out for marching columns. The British commander Sir John Maxwell stayed his hand. He had only 400 troops initially to confront roughly 1,000 insurgents and he knew he had time on his side.

The immediate priorities for the British were to amass a force of sufficient size that could guarantee the defeat of the Irish nationalist forces. On Tuesday, a British force of 4,500 men with artillery attacked and secured the Castle.

Fighting in some areas did become intense later in the week, typified by prolonged and fiercely contested hand-to-hand street battles. Military casualties were highest at Mount Street Bridge. There, newly arrived troops made successive, tactically inept, frontal attacks on determined and disciplined volunteers occupying several strongly fortified outposts. They lost 234 men, dead or wounded, while just five rebels died.

The balance was swinging decisively, however, in favour of the British because the Irish were hopelessly outnumbered. From Thursday 27th April the GPO was entirely cut off from other rebel garrisons. Next day it came under a ferocious artillery attack which also devastated much of central Dublin. Having learned the lessons of Mount Street Bridge, British troops did not attempt a mass infantry attack.

In some instances, lapses in military discipline resulted in atrocities that fuelled outrage throughout Ireland and enlisted far more solid support for the cause than had been the case before Easter 1916.

Soldiers were alleged to have killed 15 unarmed men in North King Street near the Four Courts during intense gun battles there. The British Government was never forgiven for a number of these atrocities on both sides of the Atlantic.

Overwhelming British reinforcements had been drafted efficiently into Dublin by Friday 28th April. The 1,600 nationalists - more had joined during the week - were facing around 20,000 soldiers. It compelled the insurgent leaders, based at the Post Office, first to evacuate the building and later to accept the only terms on offer, which was unconditional surrender.

The battle had lasted for seven days. Sean McDermott read out the surrender orders. The men and women wanted to fight on, but he persuaded them to accept the surrender. He told them that probably it would be just him and the other leaders who faced execution. Ireland needed the rank and file alive so they could fight another time.

He told them, "I know also that this week of Easter will never be forgotten; Ireland will one day be free because of what you've done here."

Their decision was then made known to and accepted sometimes reluctantly by all the insurgent garrisons still fighting both in the capital and in the provinces. In total the Rising cost 450 persons killed, 2,614 injured, and nine missing, almost all in Dublin.

British military casualties were 116 dead, 368 wounded and nine missing. The Irish and Dublin police forces lost 16 officers and 29 were wounded. A total of 254 civilians died; the high figures were largely because much of the fighting had occurred in or near densely populated areas.

It is widely accepted that 64 rebels lost their lives. Their casualties were low because in the capital they were the defending force. Moreover, they fought with discipline and skill until, acting under instruction from their leaders, they surrendered their strongholds rather than fight to the last volunteer.

Following a court-martial on May 9th, Sean was executed by firing squad three days later, at the age of 33. Thirteen other ringleaders were also shot during this period. Due to his disability Sean took little part in the fighting of Easter week, but was stationed at the headquarters in the General Post Office. Following the surrender he nearly escaped execution by blending in with the large body of prisoners. However, Captain Lee-Wilson, a British officer, picked out the limping man with the stick.

"Arrest him, that's the most dangerous man in Ireland after Tom Clarke!"

Shortly afterwards a sneering British officer remarked to him: "Do the Sinn Feiners take cripples in their Army?"

Reprisals against the British came eventually and in September 1919 Captain Percival Lee-Wilson, was executed in Cork on the orders of Michael Collins during the Irish War of Independence. Collins and McDermott had been close friends.

Seán MacDermott Street in Dublin is named in honour of my ancestor. So too is MacDiarmada rail station in Sligo, and Páirc Seán MacDiarmada, the Gaelic Athletic Association Stadium in Carrick-on-Shannon.

The relatives of the executed leaders asked for the bodies of their men back. They left a request form at Kilmainham jail reception before the men had been shot by the firing squad. Mrs Tom Clarke did not receive any word about her husband's body. Some of the other relatives received a letter a few weeks later to say that the bodies had already been buried. All the bodies of the executed leaders of the Rising had been covered in Quick Lime so that the entire remains would disintegrate.

The British military authorities reckoned it would be impossible to identify the bodies so that they could be given a decent burial at a later date, creating more potential flashpoints for further insurrection.

It was the way the British Government chose to try to prevent the executed men from becoming martyrs for the cause of Irish Freedom. Their action achieved the opposite of course. In burying all the men together at the Arbour Hill Prison Yard, they gave the Irish people the opportunity to create a fitting international monument to them, which it is today.

President John F Kennedy said of his visit to Ireland in June 1963, a few months before he was assassinated, that the highlight of his trip had been the memorial service at Arbour Hill Memorial Park, Dublin, where my third cousin Sean was buried in a mass grave along with thirteen other martyred ringleaders of the 1916 Uprising.

The National Monument was built in 1955 and the Proclamation of the Republic of Ireland is engraved in both Irish and English on the wall. John Kennedy was accompanied by the Taoiseach, Sean Lemass. After reviewing a Guard of Honour he walked up the pathway to the plot where the 14 men were buried. He laid a wreath of laurel and lilies to the roll of drums.

According to newspaper reports he was so impressed by the Irish military cadets that he asked for a film of the Guard of Honour drill movements to be sent to him and on his return home he suggested that a similar ceremonial drill should be introduced at the Arlington National Cemetery in Washington.

As he left Ireland at Shannon Airport he said: "This is not the land of my birth, but is the land for which I hold the greatest affection and I will certainly come back in the spring time."

He never returned to Ireland because he was slaughtered in Dallas later in the year, but Jacqueline Kennedy remembered his enthusiasm for the Irish Cadets. When making JFK's funeral arrangements she requested that Irish Army Cadets be present. They performed the same ceremonial drill at the President's funeral on November 25th 1963 as they had done in his honour at Arbour Hill.

Here is a copy of Sean's last letter written to his family the night before his execution. It shows him to be an ordinary Christian man prepared to die for what he believed in.

Kilmainham Prison
Dublin
May 11th 1916

My Dear Brothers and Sisters,

I sincerely hope that this letter will not come as a surprise to any of you, and above all that none of you will worry over what I have to say. It is just a wee note to say that I have been tried by courts martial and sentenced to be shot – to die the death of a soldier.

By the time this reaches you I will, with God's mercy, have joined in heaven, my poor father and mother as well as my dear friends who have been shot during the week......

Sean described in his letter how his comrades had acted heroically and added that he hoped when his time came in the morning he would be strong enough to share that heroism. He said he was calm and collected and felt in writing that his family was present in the cell talking to him, or taking a walk to see Mick Wayne or some of the old friends and neighbours around his home.

He said that he had had the priests with him for the past 24 hours and up to a very late hour the night before and one dear friend, the Reverend Brown Maynooth, had stayed up with him for practically 24 hours. Sean said he felt a happiness which he had never experienced in his life before and a feeling he could not describe. Knowing his state of mind he felt they should not worry or lament his fate. However, they ought not to envy him.

The cause for which he was about to die had been re-baptised during the past week by the blood of as good men who had ever trod God's earth and he was proud to be numbered among them.

Before God he wanted to assure them of how proud and happy he felt. It was not alone for himself so much that he felt happy but for the fact that Ireland had produced such men.

He stressed the importance of placing the children in positions to earn their livelihood and had faith that God would help the family to provide for each child. He wanted to pass on the message to them that he had always struck out for the practice of truth, honesty, straightforwardness in all things and sobriety. If they did this and remembered their country they would be assured a good future.

Sean emphasised the importance of the children all learning their language and history. He owned lots of books and was intending to make an arrangement with one of the priests to have these turned into a library, but he did want some kept for the children of the family.

He asked his family to take possession of the clothes he was wearing so they could be a symbol of memory and he would try to make arrangements to have them sent to his old lodgings. He mentioned a few copies of a recent photograph which could be taken and urged family to order more copies for friends. Sean was also most concerned they should speak to his old landlady in Dublin lest he owed her money and if so to pay her.

He had one more word to say about the children....he wanted some of them put to learning trades if it was possible. If any showed aptitude for mechanical or technical skills he or she should be steered in that direction. The children had been too small when he last saw them to give them that advice for it to be understood. He wanted Mary Anne to go for teaching but would lead Caty Bee and Dan to decide for her or himself. God would direct them. It ends

Make a copy of this and send it to the others as soon as you can. A lot of my friends will want to hear about me from James, Rose and Kate. They can tell them all, that in my last hours I am the same Sean they always knew and that even now I can enjoy a laugh and a joke as good as ever. I don't know if you will require a pass to get to Dublin, but you better find out before you start. Perhaps martial law will have been withdrawn before you can come; it was passed for one month only and I don't think it will be renewed.

If I think of any other things to say, I will tell them to Miss Ryan, she who in all probability, had I lived, would have been my wife. I will send on instructions, but she knows you all right. Goodbye dear brothers and sisters, make no lament for me. Pray for my soul and for my lasting pride at my death. I die that the Irish nation may live. God bless and guard you all and may the Lord have mercy on my soul.

Yours as ever,

Sean.

All my sisters had long been familiar with Co. Leitrim because, as children and adolescents, they had been taken there on holidays by Jack and Mabel. Jack and the girls apparently would always lay a wreath at the statue of Sean McDermott in Kiltyclogher, so my sisters knew much more about our third cousin than I did.

My first visit to Ireland was not until May 1999 when I was over 50. Even then I knew nothing of my illustrious ancestor, who was literally a cult figure in Ireland. I accompanied my friend Graham Thompson on a fishing trip to that part of Ireland which has some excellent Mayfly rivers including the River Boyle and Loch Corrib in Galway.

Graham is a serious and expert fisherman, unlike me, who spent his career working in the television industry where he was at one time a senior member of the production team on Central Television's *Tight Lines* which was presented by the legendary Terry Thomas. We decided to take a day off our fishing to go in hunt of my Keaney ancestors.

We arrived one morning in Glenfarne, a small town set in a valley, and I did not have to look very far to find the traces of my Keaney heartland. We parked outside a bar in the dusty main street and when I looked up I noticed the sign read *Keaney's Bar*. We knocked on the door and there was no answer. As we were getting back into the car, the bar door opened and a man came out.

"Can I help you?" he asked.

"Oh, it's all right, I was just hoping to have a drink," I replied.

"Well, we're not open till later, but come in and have a drink anyhow," was the very Irish reply.

He didn't know who we were, but served us with two pints of Guinness and pushed them in our direction.

"They're on me," he said smiling.

It was, to say the least, an overwhelming welcome and gradually I revealed who I was. In fact, he wasn't very surprised to learn that I was a Keaney, with ancestral roots in the town like him. Michael turned out to be a second cousin and he remembered Jack.

"Oh yes, the man with the limp, your Dad had a limp," he said. "There's plenty of Keaneys around here and all over the world, you'll be part of the English Keaneys."

We were soon imbibing Guinness in a big way and he wanted to phone round to bring in a few more of my relatives, and host a party for us that night. One of the locals came in at lunchtime when the bar opened and gave me a warning.

"Don't get involved with "Uncle"Keaney otherwise you'll never walk out of here, in fact you'll probably never leave Ireland."

I would have loved to have met this particular Keaney who was renowned for the "craic" and for sessions that lasted many days. Graham heard this warning and knowing my weaknesses and enjoyment of a good party eventually persuaded me that discretion was the better part of valour. We staggered out of Keaney's Bar after about two hours, early in the afternoon. We did not return for the evening session, deciding to leave a meeting with "Uncle" Keaney for another day.

We went on to meet another cousin Seamus O'Rourke at his home in Glenfarne. I'd heard about Seamus because some of my sisters stayed at his house when they were on holiday in Ireland. We knocked on his door and he turned out to be a quiet unassuming man, a non-smoking teetotaller to boot - a devout Catholic and a proper "gentleman".

He was delighted to make our acquaintance and after a chat he took us up the hill to look at the remains of the ancestral Keaney home, where my father had been raised with his nine brothers and sisters after their return from the USA. As I explained previously it had been demolished to make way for a forestry plantation and only the gable end with a hole for a window remained. A few pieces of stone were strewn around where the walls had been.

Afterwards, we went to the church in Glenfarne where my grandmother is buried with a son in the same grave, and where Sean McDermott's father may have made the pews. Seamus O'Rourke told me grandmother's grave was among the first batch dug in the churchyard in the early 1920s.

I think Graham had had enough of my ancestral search by this time and so we devoted the rest of our stay in Ireland to fishing, drinking and eating. I returned to England a stone and a half heavier than when I set out 10 days before. I caught one fish in all that time and Graham threw it back because he said it was too small to keep.

I should have enjoyed spending more time searching for the Keaney roots in Co. Leitrim in my visit in 1999, but we had agreed to go on a fishing expedition and so that is what we did.

I am yet to make the full pilgrimage in search of Sean McDermott and the ancestors, but a family reunion drawing people from different parts of the world will be staged sooner or later, and I am sure my son Justin and I will be part of that.

I am fascinated now by Sean McDermott and hungry for further information about his leading part in the 1916 Uprising. I came across this touching lament written by Seamus O'Sullivan in 1922.

They have slain you, Sean McDermott; never more these eyes will greet

The eyes beloved by women and the smile that true men loved;

Never more I'll hear the stick-tap, and the gay and limping feet

They have slain you, Sean the Gentle, Sean the valiant, Sean the proved.

Have you scorn for us who linger here behind you, Sean the wise?

As you look about and greet your comrades in the strange new dawn.

So one says, but sayings, wrongs you, for doubt never dimmed your eyes,

And not death itself could make those lips of yours grow bitter, Sean.

As your stick goes tapping down the heavenly pavement, Sean, my friend,

That is not your way of thinking, generous, tender, wise and brave;

We, who knew and loved and trusted you, are trusted to the end,

And your hand even now grips mine as though there never were a grave.

Chapter Eight

A REBEL AGAIN

By the late 1980s the hell-raising years were over and I'd matured into a genial bloke with a nice set of friends, who occasionally drank too much. I ran a small business, owned a nice comfortable house with a garage and large back garden in Brookvale Road, had a beautiful wife called Lorraine and a sturdy lad called Justin, who was doing better than I ever did at school. He seemed to prefer the round-shaped ball to the oval one, which was all right by me.

I tended to drink at the *Sportsman* in Old Town, which is called the *West End* these days. It has been gentrified, is the sort of pub you find on Richmond Hill, south west London, but still offers a great atmosphere and good dining. Other times we would meet up in the *Windmill*.

We were a mixed bunch, some educated, some not, but all practitioners in the art of self-deprecation and good humour. Our political views stretched across the spectrum from the far right to the far left which made things all the more amusing.

One of them was Terry Parks, better known as Larry the cartoonist. Terry was a socialist but we still got on very well and had many enjoyable "ding dongs". I have got several drawings he did for me about rugby and what became known as the "tour bus wars". Terry was always amused by my antics.

The drinking circle included Harry Moon and Mike Stevani, the latter a potter in town, Brian Herdman, Frank Russell, an architect and former star player for Stratford Rugby Club, Roger Smalley, "Jacko" Jackson and Colin Brook.

My other habitual haunts were the Queen's Head in Ely Street, and the back bar at the White Swan Hotel, where the town's journalists and councillors tended to congregate. Most of the scribes at the *Stratford Herald* enjoyed a drink, especially those with a background in London and Fleet Street like the sports editor Dean Bartram, my co-author Dale le Vack, Dave Maddox and his successor as local government correspondent Preston Witts.

They were encouraged by the editor Chris Towner and the arts editor Sandy Holt, especially on the night of press day. These days their favourite haunt is the *Old Thatch Tavern* which, thanks to the "colourful" nature of its clientele, has a Hogarthian touch about it.

I rediscovered my rural heritage in these years, forged with Fafa in Norfolk, by developing an interest in game shooting – this time not as a poacher but part-time as an assistant game-keeper on estates and a beater on shoots.

Game fishing in the summer months also became part of my way of life and I had the good fortune - thanks to friends - to fish rivers such as the Wye in Derbyshire, the Onny in Shropshire, and later after the millennium once a year in September, worming on the West Lyn in North Devon for salmon, staying at the *Crown Hotel* in Lynton, alcoholic haunt of wildlife artists like the late Mick Cawston.

They were often wild weekends spent with Colin Brook and Dale le Vack and other friends in company of local residents in Lynton, some of whom were men and women who took no prisoners when it came to boozing.

In Ireland I fished Loughs Corrib and Arrow and many rivers including the Boyle. I would say I am a very keen dry fly angler but have some considerable way to go before I become a master angler; a lack of patience – remark some fellow anglers - may be the problem.

Perhaps I've never lost the poacher's instincts. I do sometimes wish when I see a salmon in a pool, and that is not very often, that I had a hand grenade attached to my belt. If I had I would not hesitate to pull the pin and use it.

I joined a syndicate managing a trout lake at Upper Billesley, stocked with brown and rainbow trout, belonging to landowner and industrialist Tony Bird, who as I mentioned previously had been a successful captain and president of Stratford Rugby Club. The small lake became a haunt of roosting wild duck in the winter and a draw for the guns who were invited to shoot there.

In fact it was on Tony Bird's exclusive shoot where I rekindled my interest in pheasant, partridge and wild duck shooting, but not as a poacher. Peter Jones, Fluff's brother and an old friend from Justin's Avenue, started helping Ian Rooney, who was the gamekeeper at Upper Billesley at the time - and is now farm manager. I soon signed up to helping Ian as well and realised what I had been missing all these years since the 1960s.

The shoot had previously been owned by Bob Ansell of the brewing family, but it had fallen into decline during his final years at the big house - and so we had to work hard to restore it to its former glory, with good access to the sky from the ground for the guns.

We started rearing day-old pheasant chicks until they were old enough to be transferred into pens in the woods, where they were fed to grow on. As they matured they were able to leave the sanctuary by flying over the protective fencing and venturing into the wild.

When the birds are still small chicks, and even as young pheasant, the job requires your time seven evenings a week and you can't have a night off. We were feeding, watering, tidying up, doing brush cutting and making the estate presentable for the visitors at weekends.

On the day of the shoot I was one of the beaters. The job is to flush the pheasants towards the guns. It becomes a practised art – you know where the birds are in the wood and you get in a straight line and walk forward, steadily tapping your stick until you get to the flushing points.

The object is to disturb the birds so they take off in great fright and get reasonably high over the waiting guns to provide the best sport. The art is in providing what is known as a "testing bird" which means it is difficult to shoot. Earlier in the season the birds may still be relatively tame and unused to being fired upon. They have a tendency to scuttle off through the undergrowth rather than getting airborne. The job becomes less difficult after the New Year, when the adult birds have become very wary of shooting parties and will fly off at speed.

The Upper Billesley shoot was an exclusive one and Tony Bird was friendly with top industrialists and politicians who were frequent visitors. Everything was done properly, which is the way it should be, because shooting can be an extremely dangerous sport without the discipline and protocol that must go with it. We beaters did not see much of the big names during the day usually, but they were all very nice to us when we did meet them.

I was a poacher turned gamekeeper and it amused me because when I was a youngster in Norfolk all the people standing on the gun-pegs to shoot driven pheasants were either "toffs" or very rich people. I never ever thought that one day in later life I would be standing on a gun-peg myself. A lot of other working people who have taken up shooting will tell you the same thing.

I'll never forget my first invitation to be a gun on the Upper Billesley shoot. I have kept the invitation card that Tony Bird sent me. I arrived at the big house for coffee and was greeted by Tony and Janet and introduced to the other guests who included the eight guns. I was nervous but soon put at ease by their friendly and outward-going manner. We were transported to the first of the three drives for the morning across the estate.

Then it was back by Range Rover to a fantastic lunch cooked personally by Janet Bird, who wouldn't have it any other way. There were two more drives in the afternoon and it was back for tea to the big house. I have always been a good shot thanks to my childhood and I acquitted myself well– and wasn't embarrassed by doing anything that would be frowned upon as a breach of etiquette, like shooting someone else's bird.

I thought of Fafa often that day and had a strong feeling he was all around me having a good chuckle at the spectacle of young Danny mingling with the "toffs" on his own gun-peg without so much as the "doff" of his cap. I think he would have been proud of the way he trained me.

Since that day I have been fortunate enough to be invited to shoot on several estates and it now feels completely natural for me to participate on equal terms with others. It is a sport that has become accessible to the budget of far more working people than in the 1950s when I used to follow Fafa in his wake, as he carried his ancient and rusty Belgian shotgun furtively through the woods.

I am still a beater on various shoots, even though I am now in my 60s and will continue to do it until the phone stops ringing. I am a beater and occasionally a gun on a friend's shoot in the Cotswolds and still help to look after the young pheasants on a family-owned estate with wooded hills at Haselor, near Stratford, where Steve Talbot is game-keeper and I am also a beater there. Shooting and beating satisfies all my instincts in a big way as a countryman, and perhaps indeed as a frustrated farmer.

There is nothing better than getting up very early of a morning when everybody else is asleep and venturing off into the darkness - and then being in the wood or out in the fields as the sun rises. It gives you a sense of freedom, a sense of being at one with nature and a witness to what is going on in the wild. It is a time to see deer and foxes moving about, buzzards on patrol in the sky and pigeons coming off the roost.

During these years in the late 1980s, to the middle of the 1990s, I was also an enthusiastic follower on foot of the Warwickshire and Croome and West Warwickshire Hunts. I would also venture out to the Raven Hotel at Droitwich in Worcestershire sometimes to follow the hounds.

I loved the ambience of the occasions, the excitement and anticipation and being out in the open countryside. Hunting for me expressed perfectly the ritual aspect of the English rural way of life and what is wonderful about it.

Unfortunately, some working men and women saw it entirely as a class thing and resented it for that reason – but I knew ordinary country people loved to go hunting too and it provided employment, pleasure and lifelong friendships as a whole way of life. Socially I was never really part of it, except for the puppy shows which I enjoyed, and certainly hunt balls are not my scene.

It's the reality that counts and the reality is that between 6,000 and 8,000 full time jobs depend on hunting in the UK, of which about 700 jobs result from direct hunt employment and 1,500 to 3,000 come from indirect employment on hunting-related activities.

In the UK, supporters of fox hunting regard it as a distinctive part of British culture generally, the basis of traditional crafts and a key part of social life in rural areas, an activity and spectacle enjoyed not only by the riders but also by others like me whether on foot, bicycle or Land Rover

I see hunting as an extraordinarily visual experience if you know how to be in the right place at the right time. If you are, then the sight of the huntsman with the hounds at a critical moment, working the hedgerows and the fields, or an experienced rider taking his or her horse over an enormous hedge, perhaps not knowing what is on the other side, is an unforgettable experience.

The hunt itself began when hounds were cast into rough or brushy areas called coverts, where foxes often laid up during daylight hours, or when they heard hounds moving toward them. If the pack managed to pick up the scent of a fox, they would track it for as long as they were able.

Scenting can be affected by temperature, humidity, and other factors. The hounds pursue the trail and the riders follow, by the most direct route possible which, as I have mentioned, may involve very athletic skill on the part of horse and rider alike.

The hunt continued until either the fox evaded the hounds, went to ground (taking refuge in an underground burrow or den) or was overtaken and usually killed by the hounds. Where the fox went to ground it might have been dug out and killed, often using terriers to locate it.

Through my years of being a hunt supporter I have always been aware of the vociferous nature of the anti-hunting lobby, supported by the RSPCA. I have respected their point of view, provided they did not try to disrupt hunting activities through ill-mannered interference. In such cases when I did come across hunts being subverted I took a dim view of it.

One Boxing Day I attended a Worcestershire Hunt meeting at the Raven Hotel where a large group of anti-hunting activists had gathered to try and disrupt it. I found myself confronted by two activists, one dressed as a fox and the other as a badger. One of them threw a tin of paint at me that missed, but I was left with no alternative but to go back and confront them.

I grabbed hold of the fox and lifted him off the ground so that his whiskers were touching my chin and his back paws were off the ground, his brush trailing along the ground.

"Get your hands off me, I don't know where you've been," he sneered somewhat nervously. It made things worse for him, of course, and he had to have a good slap. The badger did not intervene to help his friend the fox - and was lucky to escape similar retribution. I went home and had a laugh about it with Lorraine. Later that evening we were having a drink watching television when there was a knock on the door and two policemen were standing outside on the porch.

"We've had a complaint from two members of the public – one dressed as a fox and the other as a badger - that they were assaulted and manhandled by you Sir," said one of the policemen. I explained what had happened and the policemen were actually quite amused by it. No action was taken.

Unfortunately, as the 1990s progressed, the actions of those who stood against hunting became much more militant and aggressive and a majority of Labour MPs saw it wrongly as a class issue that needed to be dealt with on that basis. The anti-hunt lobby was gaining powerful friends in and out of parliament.

By early 1997 Labour were favourites to win the General Election to be held in May. The British economy had been in recession during the 1992 election, which the Conservatives had won, and although the recession had ended within a year, events such as the Tory Government's reputation for economic management had been tarnished.

Labour was leading the way in the polls a long time before the death of its leader John Smith in May 1994, after which Tony Blair became leader. Despite the strong economic recovery and substantial fall in unemployment in the four years leading up to the election, the rise in Tory support was only marginal, with all of the major opinion polls showing Labour in a comfortable lead.

The UK general election was held on 1st May and the Labour Party under Tony Blair won it in a landslide victory with 418 seats, the most seats the party has ever held. This marked the beginning of the longest period of time in government ever for the Labour Party. That year, Tony Blair declared himself to be opposed to hunting and promised a Bill to outlaw it. It was a pledge to end fox-hunting – he'd actually live to regret it.

I was seeing red mist again by now. New Labour was the enemy and Danny was about to become a rebel and outlaw once more, this time a middle-age rebel and outlaw. How dare these bastards interfere with something they knew nothing about? As far as I was concerned the main reason for them doing it was that they hated the people who took part in hunting, whether it was "toffs" on horseback or the rural workers who followed on foot, like Charlie Baker my grandfather.

He was one of those people who fought for his freedom - and one of his freedoms was being able to do what he liked in the countryside. As far as I was concerned those bastards were not going to get away with it. It was as simple as that. I was going to make sure that those New Labour shits would know they'd been in a fight.

The first mass rally to defend hunting was organised by the Countryside Alliance in Hyde Park when Labour had been in power for some months. The programme brochure for the day, handed out to thousands of people, told Countryside Alliance supporters what the focus of the rally was:

- *The countryside needs country sports.*

- *Country sports are the test case for the political future of rural areas.*

- *We are winning the argument on the giant contribution that country sports make to the economy.*

- *Employment and conservation underwrite the welfare of animal species.*

- *In politics no one wins just by being right. People win by being strong.*

- *We must establish now with a massive show of numbers that country interests cannot be overruled by politicians who choose not to listen to facts but listen instead to interests that are hostile to specific aspects of rural life.*

- *Strong support for country sports now will ensure for the future of equestrian sports, shooting, fishing, farming, hunting and the country way of life.*

- *All these things are now at risk from the same small faction with its moral megaphone.*

The Countryside Alliance followed this up with a further wave of protest demonstrations and marches every few months in the following years. Nearly 300,000 people marched through London and a year later nearly half a million took to the streets in Britain's biggest demo ever to defend the rural way of life.

One of the most spectacular demonstrations accompanied the Hunting Bill as it went before the House of Lords for its second reading in September 2003. Activists transformed the rural landscape into a sea of red and green - red for anger, green for the countryside - with waves of posters, banners and car stickers.

Foxhounds and beagles invaded the Piazza at London's Covent Garden as their dog handlers lobbied metropolitan passers-by about how our livelihood and way of life would be under threat if any ban became law. I continued to attend these good-natured and peaceful rallies while the issue of hunting rumbled on in the Commons and the Lords.

Meanwhile the anti-hunt activists, egged on by New Labour MPs like John Prescott, had the scent of victory in their nostrils and were becoming even more militant and vociferous in their disruption of the sport. It was clear they saw it in terms of being a class issue and only a minority cared about the so-called cruelty factor.

There was a detectable arrogance in their expression, a deeply patronising and dismissive attitude towards the pro-hunt lobby. They wanted to deride a traditional way of life that had been part of England, Scotland, Wales and Ireland for hundreds of years on the basis that they, the chattering urban classes, were always right, better educated and knew better than us countryside "toss-pots".

All I could see were sneering faces of the New Labour ministers and back-benchers and I really thought that we had to up the ante. Not unexpectedly, more militant factions in the Countryside Alliance now began to emerge, some more than happy to bend the law. In 2004 there was a massive demonstration when hundreds of thousands of hunt supporters in massed ranks confronted riot police outside the Houses of Parliament. During that protest a group of hunt supporters invaded Parliament, which posed all sorts of questions about the efficiency of the security services.

One foolish but tiny breakaway organisation called itself the Real Countryside Alliance - aping in bad taste the Irish terrorist group and causing deep embarrassment within the Countryside Alliance. The ranks of the RCA included a handful of hunt supporters who began to threaten the sabotage of essential services, including electricity pylons, gas supplies and articulated trucks carrying food for supermarkets.

They talked darkly about disrupting railways and telephone lines, dumping sand into sewers to block drains, immobilising a motorway by covering it with rivets that would slash tyres. This tiny faction even whispered in the shadows about "terrorist-style attacks" on government offices by extremists divided, like the IRA, into unconnected impenetrable cells.

The self-styled Real Countryside Alliance launched with a huge poster on one of the most visible and expensive billboards in London with an accompanying 7,000 fly-poster campaign depicting a freed balaclava-clad terrorist beside an imprisoned hunt member. Their aims were unrealistic, but the tiny group knew how to tweak Fleet Street to grab the headlines.

The majority of militants disagreed with the RCA. Threats to reservoirs, power and gas supplies, and disrupting food supplies to supermarkets would be totally unacceptable and ninety-nine per cent of it was just pub talk. It was at this time that some people decided to stay in the Countryside Alliance, but also to become members of the more hard line Countryside Action Network, which led the motorway tractor convoys. There was nothing illegal, the CAN leaders pointed out correctly, about placing slow-moving convoys of farm vehicles on motorways or across every bridge in London.

Janet George, the main media spokesperson for CAN, predicted hunting would continue whatever happened in Parliament. A national newspaper quoted her as saying: "We'll restructure it to make policing of hunting unworkable."

Hunts would become co-operatives so that there were no leaders to prosecute. Everyone would carry a horn. Ownership of kennels might be put in offshore trusts. Each hound would be made a child's pet. Farmers would sign declarations that only legal hunting would be allowed on their land. If the police came, everyone would hand over their horse and hound. It would therefore be impossible for police forces to cope.

I was impressed by Peter Gent, Peter Hole and Janet George of CAN, if not some of the other self-styled militants who threatened more than they delivered. After three years of taking the middle road with the Countryside Alliance I also joined the Countryside Action Network, many of whose members remained in the Countryside Alliance.

I agreed that it was now necessary to up the ante and take much more direct action to show New Labour we meant business – block more motorways, block London off and confront anti-hunting MPs wherever they went. We felt the campaign needed more teeth and militancy, but it would have to be sensible direct action that would not have CAN members labelled as terrorists. We did do all those things just mentioned and became a force to be reckoned with.

Instead of just walking round with banners, having picnics, sharing a bottle of Chablis and singing songs no one was listening to, we felt we needed a cutting edge to show the Government what we could do. We needed to ram home the clearest message to the Labour Government that by direct action we could bring the country to a standstill, for example by closing down the motorway network again and again whenever we wanted.

Peter Gent, one of CAN's founders recalls: "We were utterly demoralised by the lack of activity and strategy inside the Countryside Alliance to try and defend hunting for generations to come. Peter Hole and I decided that the only way to do that would be an action group rather than a talking group that would actually do things that would dramatically increase the general public's awareness of how strongly hunting people felt about the continuation of their activities and their interest in their sport.

"We formed CAN late in 2001 and we published application forms to all and sundry throughout Great Britain. We were almost overwhelmed initially by people who wanted to do something – rather than talk about doing something. We asked Janet George to be our face and voice to the media. We also identified a number of key people in various locations around the UK who could be the leading activists in their area to encourage others in the fraternity and follow the strategy we were trying to put together – one of course in the Midlands was Danny."

So I became a leading member of the Warwickshire Committee of the Countryside Action Network and I played a role in organising direct action on its behalf over the next few years, whether these were demonstrations, intercepting Government ministers to embarrass them in public, or disrupting motorway traffic.

We met every month in secret and even now the minutes of those meetings are secret and will remain so. I felt it was something I had to do because it was a cause I believed in passionately, even though Lorraine was not happy about my involvement - and Justin my son warned me it was causing her great distress.

She was having sleepless nights because she was frightened that I was going to get myself locked up. In the end, she accepted it was something I would not walk away from. My friends in the CAN organisation also knew and accepted that Special Branch and probably even MI5 were building up personal files on the more militant activists joining the Countryside Action Network, but there was no going back for us. We felt we were defending our way of life.

Over the years following the millennium I took part regularly in demonstrations to support the hunting issue and was always at the forefront when this involved confrontation – whether with anti-hunt activists, New Labour MPs or of course the police, who had the unenviable job of controlling the crowds at demonstrations.

I was cautioned, manhandled roughly and arrested many times by the police at the barriers but remained undeterred. Looking back, I think I was extremely fortunate never to have been charged with an offence which would have ended up with me behind bars.

Charged with tension as these incidents always were at demonstrations, I have to say that sometimes they were also extremely amusing with their lighter moments. Bob Hemming from Alcester had been a friend for many years and in his youth during the 1960s and 1970s made his name as a leading rugby player for Stratford RFC Coventry and Moseley RFC.

Bob supported the Croome and West Warwickshire Hunt, took part in its activities, and agreed to accompany me down to Whitehall to attend a pro-hunt demonstration at 3.00pm outside the Houses of Parliament, to coincide with one of the readings of the Bill. He thought we were just going along to attend the demonstration but he had no idea there was a plan by the leaders of CAN to cause severe disruption to the traffic. We knew it would certainly bring us into conflict with the police but poor old Bob was oblivious to this.

The Square began to fill up with pro-hunt supporters on foot, most carrying placards and chanting. None of our cars was marked with pro-hunting Countryside Alliance stickers and badges - so we hoped we could keep the police guessing on the wrong foot. I was sorry by then that I had got Bob involved in it, but I needed someone to advise me how to get to Parliament Square without getting lost. He had become a hunt activist for the day.

Bob first became rather alarmed when the lights turned to green in the Square and instead of moving forward I turned off the ignition and just sat there with a straight face. Traffic behind us immediately began stacking up and irate drivers honked their horn in irritation.

"For fuck's sake Danny we can't just sit here, we've got to move with the traffic! You'll get yourself arrested!" he exclaimed.

"That's why we're here mate," I told him for the first time. I said nothing else and a further two or three minutes elapsed as traffic chaos began to reign in Parliament Square as a result of what I and other activists in cars were doing. Bob was looking around him like a demented meerkat.

"Danny you can't do this, you're going to get us bloody arrested any moment!" he pleaded.

"That would be good," I replied with a smile and Bob uttered a succession of expletives at what he considered to be my bloody-mindedness. I started drinking from a bottle of water, quite unconcerned at the chaos around us.

Things did not develop any further in Parliament Square unfortunately, because a few minutes later the police closed it for the duration of the protest demonstration, as there were by now thousands of people on foot, chanting and carrying banners daubed with slogans.

I was waved on by the police to cross Westminster Bridge and reluctantly moved off followed by a long line of highly irate drivers. I drove deliberately slowly across the bridge with Bob looking back in embarrassment at the stacked up traffic. What happened next, however, was the last straw for him.

A black Jaguar was approaching slowly across the bridge coming from the opposite direction - and some instinct told me to cut across in front of it, to slow it right down. I could see it was definitely a Government car and so might be carrying a Cabinet Minister. This was a dream opportunity for me to unleash some verbal harassment – the kind I relished, and the sort of situation - from the look on his face - that Bob abhorred. The Jaguar slowed down to a crawl and our two cars stopped and touched wing mirrors.

I peered into the back seat before hurriedly winding down the front window. Tony Blair was sitting there in the corner going through some notes. He hadn't taken in the situation and didn't look up until he heard me shouting at him.

"You fucking wanker, Blair. You and your new fucking Labour are entirely responsible for all this mess. Leave the countryside alone. You should be fucking ashamed at yourself, you tosser!" I screamed, perhaps not choosing my words with great elegance, because the red mist had submerged me in the excitement of the moment.

By now Bob was crapping himself. He was curled up almost in a foetal position trying very hard not to be there - with most of his body concealed from view below the passenger window. I heard him hiss behind his hand.

"Now you fucking well have done it - you bloody idiot Keaney. It's the sodding Prime Minister. You've just called him a fucking wanker for Christ's sake."

Tony Blair looked up from his notes, obviously heard what I had to say, and seemed to half acknowledge me, before the Jaguar sped away across the bridge in the direction of Parliament. I drove triumphantly across the bridge having successfully given the arch enemy, the grand satan, a piece of my mind, even if I had chosen my words somewhat carelessly on the spur of the moment.

I was chuckling, but Bob was mute; his face a lighter shade of pale. I turned left to head back towards Whitehall. Suddenly I noticed an unmarked Vauxhall car pull out of a turning behind me. It shot past our car and forced me to stop. I slammed on the brakes to avoid a collision.

There was a strange muted humming sound, a bit like a baby sucking its thumb, coming from Bob. Two plain-clothes men got out of the Vauxhall and one of them pushed his head through the still-open window on the driver's side. His head loomed large in front of mine and he gave me a derisory smile. I remember his breath smelled of peppermint.

"Good afternoon Mr Keaney. What are you doing?"

"I'm sight-seeing," I told him.

"Fuck off back to Stratford!" He warned.

I was content to let him have the last word and to drive off, not to Stratford, but to rejoin the demonstration still going on in Parliament Square. Fuck 'em.

Things got very nasty at another demonstration not long afterwards when the police seemed to be on a short fuse and several pro-hunt demonstrators got hit over the head. I was at the front by a police barrier looking across to the Houses of Parliament and had my foot on the bottom rung.

"Get your foot off the barrier," a policeman told me.

"Fuck off, there's no law against it," I replied.

The next thing I was hauled over the barrier roughly like a rag doll by two or three of them and found myself lying on the road with them standing over me.

"You go on like that and we'll arrest you for obstruction. Now get out of here," one of the coppers shouted.

Obligingly I made myself scarce and rejoined the demonstration at the back, taking care to avoid the same group of policemen. You never gave in – you just carried on and risked arrest. I was hauled out like that several times and warned, but always got away with it.

On another occasion I was walking back after the demonstration to my car carrying a placard attached to some two-by-two timber. It accused the Government of ethnically cleansing country people – relevant because it was the time when Tony Blair and US President Bill Clinton had been in Bosnia trying to find a solution to the war there and stop the ethnic cleansing. There was a long queue of traffic because of the demo and a lorry was caught in it near the back of the queue – its driver was fuming. He just happened to direct his derogatory remark in my direction.

"Why don't you fuck off back to your manor house!" he sneered in a thick cockney accent as he stuck his head out of the window.

"Why don't you fuck off back to your shithouse," I replied.

I decided I'd show him what was on the banner to shut him up - and as I unfolded it I pushed it up towards his cab window. Unfortunately, by accident, the end of the timber caught him right on the nostril and made his nose bleed. There was a line of coppers over the other side of the road and they had seen the wood catch him on the nostril.

"Oh shit, if they'll think it did deliberately they'll nick me," I heard myself saying.

The cockney truck driver opened the cab door, jumped out and called over to the coppers, clutching his nose.

"Arrest that bastard, he's just assaulted me!"

A policeman sauntered over, tapped him on the shoulder and said to him: "Next time you keep your fucking nose out of it!"

Tony Blair was not the only leading New Labour figure I came across during my years as a hunt activist – I also encountered Lord Whitty, Parliamentary Under-Secretary of State at Defra and also the Deputy Prime Minister John Prescott, who will never know how close he came to getting his head knocked off his shoulders - I wanted to knock that notorious sneer off his face.

Lord Larry Whitty of Camberwell in the London Borough of Southwark had special responsibility for Farming, Food and Sustainable Energy. Made a life peer in 1996, he was an irresistible New Labour target for me with his urban public school background, Cambridge degree in economics and an earlier career as a "mover and shaker" with both the TUC and the General Municipal Boilermakers and Allied Trade Union. In my view, Larry Whitty was a classic example of the chattering classes – I saw him as a socialist "townie" who considered he knew better than those of us living in the countryside. I couldn't wait to ruin his day.

The Countryside Action Network had been tipped off that Lord Whitty was due to visit Oxford and we were also told when and where he was going to be there. I made it my business to be in Oxford when he was - as part of our ongoing strategy to harrass and embarrass New Labour Government ministers.

It was the sort of task I particularly enjoyed, but he caught us on the wrong foot by getting out of a taxi instead of a Government car. It meant we had to change our tactics at a moment's notice. He approached the building on foot where he had a meeting scheduled. As he started going up the steps I decided on the spur of the moment to step forward and block his progress. I didn't touch his lordship with my hands - because the police were there and they would probably have arrested me for assault or something even worse.

Instead, I rushed forward and by sticking out my chest I managed to bump him back down the steps. Lord Whitty had two minders with him, both of whom were bloody useless and I soon pushed them out of the way. They were a couple of real dorks who tried to stop me doing it - but were easily brushed aside. I had my own minder in the form of big Dave Hawkins so I felt quite safe.

I made my views clearly and loudly known and then the police stepped in and formed a screen around the Minister so that he could go into his scheduled meeting. I can't remember what I said to him as I "chested" him down the steps, but I'm sure I said it loudly enough. He actually looked quite scared at one point and I could not help but ask myself why we were allowing such nonentities to try and screw up our way of life.

Deputy Prime Minister John Prescott was made of sterner stuff to give him his due. He came to Stratford to visit Shakespeare's Birthplace and the Shakespeare Centre in Henley Street shortly before he was involved in the famous egg-throwing incident in North Wales when he threw a punch at a hunt supporter. I was determined to get him because the previous week he had talked in public in a speech about the contorted faces of the Countryside Alliance.

As a member of the Alliance I had taken great exception to his words and then to my great surprise and delight read in the *Herald* that he was about to visit my home town. I was waiting for him outside the Shakespeare Centre when he came out with his attractive PA and three or four minders.

"Oi, Prescott!" I shouted from the other side of the street. His bodyguards did not want him to come over, but he walked over to me anyway.

"What's this shit about the contorted face of the Countryside Alliance then?" I asked him angrily. It was obvious to passers-by that a verbal fracas was brewing and a crowd quickly collected around us.

"It was taken out of context," he replied gruffly in his Northern accent.

"No it fucking wasn't, because I was there when you said it," I told him.

"Anyway, I think hunting is cruel and we're going to ban it, make no mistake about it," he said even more gruffly.

"Have you ever been hunting?" I asked.

"No, but I don't have to. It involves cruelty to animals. Getting animals to kill other animals and that's cruel isn't it!"

"Well if you've never been fucking hunting how come you know so much about it?" I asked contemptuously.

"It's just a class thing for you, isn't it! You can't stand the people who do it, can you!"

By now he was beginning to get annoyed too and all I wanted to do was punch the fucking twat in the face and wipe that sneering look off it. My heart was pounding so loudly I could hear it. I had to restrain myself. I knew it would land me in real trouble if I "twatted" him – after all, he was the Deputy Prime Minister. I desperately wanted to knock his fat head off his shoulders, but I knew I could not put my family through the notoriety that would go with it.

Actually, I'll give Prescott the credit for having the guts to come up to a big bloke like me whose body language must have made it quite clear I was spoiling for an argument. He does have guts, I'll give him that – and maybe that's why I let him have the last word, as his minders came over to collect him. As he walked off he turned and said: "Oi, I suppose you're the happy face of the Countryside Alliance!"

Tony Blair has recently revealed that he didn't want either side to be a clear winner in this dangerous dispute that was dividing the country – what he wanted was a solution that would enable both sides to claim victory with reasonable justification. According to the Countryside Alliance, since the act came into force in 2005, only a handful of hunts have been successfully prosecuted.

He now goes on the record that he deliberately sabotaged the ban on fox hunting, calling it "one of the domestic legislative measures I most regret." In his book *A Journey* he admits he ensured that the 2004 Hunting Act was "a masterly British compromise" that left enough loopholes to allow hunting to continue "provided certain steps were taken to avoid cruelty when the fox is killed."

He also told Home Office minister Hazel Blears to steer the police away from enforcing the law. Ironically, Blair's 1997 pledge to give Parliament a vote on the subject dogged him throughout his time in office, with lawmakers opposed to hunting repeatedly trying to introduce a ban.

"The passions aroused by the issue were primeval," he writes. "If I'd proposed solving the pension problem by compulsory euthanasia for every fifth pensioner I'd have got less trouble. By the end of it, I felt like the damn fox."

"I won a bet with the Prince of Wales," Blair writes. "He thought the ban was absurd, and raised the issue with me in a slightly pained way. The wager was that after I left office, people would still be hunting."

To his credit, Blair now admits he initially agreed to a ban without properly understanding the issue. Then, during a vacation in Italy, he found himself talking to the master of a hunt near Oxford.

"She took me calmly and persuasively through what they did, the jobs that were dependent on it, the social contribution of keeping the hunt and the social consequence of banning it, and did it with an effect that completely convinced me," he says.

In hindsight I have no doubt that a shrewd politician like Blair could see the cruelty issue would eventually lead to the lunatic fringe in organisations like the Animal Liberation Front moving against shooting, fishing and traditional working men's activities like ferreting and hunting rabbits. There would be nothing for New Labour in going down that route.

I also have no doubt that those who pursued the course of direct action like the Countryside Action Network played a significant role in achieving the end result that we did. The Countryside Alliance was immense in holding the middle ground and everything else together. Clare Rowson and Nicky Driver, Midland organisers for the Countryside Alliance, did a great job in my opinion, but rough diamonds like me opened a Pandora's Box for many politicians who saw the issue as potentially one that could divide Britain and do great damage to the fabric of our society.

I totally forgive one of the Masters of the Warwickshire Hunt for calling me - and blokes like me - hotheads, (I understand) but actually the Alliance needed us, even though they thought we'd give hunting a bad name. We were actually the cutting edge of the campaign.

Peter Gent, the most energetic and passionate of the masterminds behind CAN recalls those campaigning years: "We were trying to convince Joe Public that we were not only earnest in our wishes, but that we were also to some extent prepared to commit ourselves in a way that perhaps wouldn't have been thought of previously.

"There were a number of major demonstrations in Parliament Square that we either called, or were part of. On more than one occasion in Parliament Square I and many hundreds of others were violently attacked by riot police, with no obvious numbers on their epaulettes. Our mobile phones were under surveillance too, so our movements could be tracked and even our exact location revealed - but we found ways of dealing with that.

"We staged a motorway blockade on five different motorways merely to show that we could do it. We picketed the Defra offices in London on at least two occasions, specifically aimed at its head, Alun Michael, whom we couldn't believe the Countryside Alliance was prepared to trust.

"In fact, we were involved in the harassment of ministers all over the UK and one year we tried to disrupt the Labour Party Conference in a significant way in Blackpool, but the main ringleaders were arrested by riot police carrying sub-machine guns prior to the event.

"Danny was highly respected by his fellow members of CAN. I recall an incident in Parliament Square where every time I looked around he was in front of me forging his way towards the front of the barricades. I can remember also packing down with him rugby style in an effort to attempt - with many hundreds of others – to break our way through the barricades.

"I have always thought of Danny as being my number one sidekick, because whatever you wanted Danny to do he didn't usually question why, he just assumed what he was doing - and what he was being asked to do - was for the general benefit of the movement and of hunting in general. For that, I shall be eternally grateful to Danny."

The Bus Wars...

My years as a leading hunt activist stood me in good stead during the summer of 2001 when the peace of Brookvale Road - and much of hitherto undisturbed residential Shottery - was suddenly shattered without warning or consultation by the arrival of open-topped double-decker buses being driven down our road full of gawping sight-seers on their way to Ann Hathaway's Cottage. The "bus-wars" as they came to be known were upon us.

We knew of the Guide Friday double-deckers, which did not use our road as a thoroughfare to Ann Hathaway's cottage, but the new invasion was mounted by its new competition in Stratford, a much more aggressive company from London, called City Sightseeing.

One morning an open-top City Sightseeing bus appeared in Brookvale Road, followed by another, and then another. In fact they were arriving one every 10 minutes. I wrote down the phone number printed on the side of one of the buses as it went past my home and rang their head office. A rather superior-sounding bloke came on the line.

"Yes, we are now operating in Stratford and we have a licence to do so legally," he said curtly, as if that was the end of the matter. He mentioned his company City Sightseeing was providing a service in opposition to a local competitor Guide Friday.

I told him: "This is a residential road and you are disturbing the peace here with those open-top buses coming through every few minutes. It is not acceptable and furthermore you have not even consulted us about it." There was rising anger in my voice.

"Well, there is nothing you can do about it. The licence has been obtained and it's all legal and above board. Our route has been approved by Warwickshire County Council highways department, the police and the local district council. If you were not informed it's not our fault. Sorry, but there's nothing you can do about it. We are here to stay."

Those words brought on the red mist and I saw them as a direct threat and a challenge. These people were going to degrade our way of life as if we did not matter – in fact we might as well not even exist as far as they were concerned. We would have to take direct action to stop them – something I was not worried about doing, having been at it since 1997 as a hunt activist.

"Well you might bloody well think it's all sewn up and you're here to stay mate, but I can tell you that you're not going to use Brookvale Road - and that is an absolute promise."

I slammed down the phone, had a think for a few minutes and came to the conclusion that Brookvale Road would have to get organised as a community to fight this at once and without any further delay.

I found a superb ally in the shape of Irena Johnson, and her husband Russell, who lived on the corner of Evesham Road and Brookvale Road. Irena had been enjoying the fresh air in her back garden when the first of the open-top buses carrying its gawking load of passengers, the Oriental ones armed with cameras, disturbed her peace, followed by several more passenger cargoes of the same, within the space of a couple of hours.

She was incandescent with rage and within half an hour we were talking and planning - and even my normally shy and retiring wife Lorraine was scheming with us. The management of City Sightseeing would live to regret the day they invaded the privacy of Irena Johnson. She was a formidable foe for them and made an ideal partner for someone like me, who was used to taking direct action.

Everyone else in the road rallied round enthusiastically and we formed a committee within 24 hours to organise the resistance. There were several key members. These hard-liners included Richard and Zoe Biggs, pensioners Beryl and Barbara who were both widows in their 70s, Lilly Hira, Bernard and Gary Mills, and a lady called Maggie. Tony and Jean Savage were rocks, as were Steve and Angie Webster---there were many more including Irena and Russell's son Oliver who was soon making placards to display outside his house.

We agreed unanimously that direct action was the only course of action that was going to work. We would have to be decisive and prepared if necessary for a sustained campaign without dropping our guard. Brookvale Road would have to be blocked off every day so that the buses could not use it.

That is exactly what happened and for several weeks through the summer and into the early autumn the company tried to get through Brookvale Road and into other parts of Shottery but were never able to do so. We found a way to park the cars so that private vehicles could just get through by taking care – but not larger ones.

On some days City Sightseeing buses were stacked back for hundreds of yards along Evesham Road and there were angry scenes around and outside our homes and also down in Shottery, even outside Ann Hathaway's Cottage, as drivers, conductors and then company officials tried to intervene. There was much swearing and insulting but never physical violence.

The *Stratford Herald* reporters and photographers led by David Maddox and Mark Williamson had a field day – it was such a visual story with real confrontation between the two sides and the hapless passengers caught in the middle. It hit Fleet Street and even went international because of the Shakespeare connection.

The company warned us, threatened us with legal action, with being arrested by the police and carted off into custody - and in shrill tones they waved licences and signed agreements from so-called authorities in our faces. I had heard it all before, of course, even if my neighbours had not, but we all laughed and said we could not care less.

The solidarity was nothing short of marvellous. Direct action is so often the only effective weapon of the people. If somebody interferes with your life then you hit back and you interfere with theirs. You make them think - and we did make them think by blocking off all the routes except one to the historic cottage. Thousands of visitors to the Shakespeare houses were affected.

We arranged the road blocks expertly and when the police arrived to tell us to move the cars, and warn us of arrest if we continued what we were doing there, another road block a few hundred yards up or down the road near Ann Hathaway's Cottage would suddenly materialise. As there were just a handful of policemen on duty at any one time in the Stratford area, they just didn't stand a chance. These were perfect guerrilla tactics.

We also had some "inkling" that some of the local policemen were not unsympathetic to our cause.

We became experts in blockading and just refused to be intimidated. We knew we needed to be patient, because time was on our side. We were quoted in the newspapers warning that we would go on doing it all year if we had to, until the weather was too cold for open-top buses.

City Sightseeing was getting nothing but bad publicity from it all and its passengers clearly did not want to be part of the confrontation – or indeed the longish walk that became necessary when their bus reached a barrier and could go no further. We knew many of the tourists were intimidated by the strength of feeling of the residents, because virtually every car in Shottery had a sticker expressing solidarity with our cause, every house window a poster – as did every street lamp and telegraph pole. It must have been disastrous for their business.

At weekends we would specifically target the road down to Ann Hathaway's cottage, knowing this would cause extreme chaos. We even mounted demonstrations in the town centre and blocked off roads there with cars. Eventually we enlisted the support of two councillors, Juliet Short and Giovanni Renna, who spoke up for us at full district council and committee meetings. Town councillor Mick Crutchley was also a great help.

Eventually it came down to talks with Terry Gabrielle, a director of City Sightseeing who asked us to negotiate with them. Actually, he was a very nice bloke and he was a good listener, but we knew he was in a position where he did not really have a lot of choice. We had made it clear we could spring road blocks every day of the week until the cows came home.

We had widened the conflict to underline our resolution by starting to block off the lanes to Wilmcote where Mary Arden's Cottage was a major Shakespeare attraction. We would drive selected cars in a line at a snail's pace along the lane. This soon had the buses stacking up behind them. We would let through local people in their cars so as not to annoy the villagers. This tactic really scared City Sightseeing because it was now serious disruption to their business on an entirely different route.

Terry Gabrielle came to my house one Friday afternoon and I took him to the Bell Inn, the famous pub on the traffic island in Shottery. We sat outside in the beer garden and had a beer while I showed him that his buses had to mount the pavement in order to get round a very sharp corner. As far as we were concerned it was this which made the road entirely unsuitable for buses. It was the straw that broke the camel's back--- that and Irena's forceful personality. He knew for definite then his company would lose any appeal or court action on grounds of safety. Terry did want to ease the situation and we thanked him for his sensible and professional contribution.

He agreed reluctantly to withdraw the open-top buses from the routes to which we objected and to use another route instead. City Sightseeing would re-route their vehicles through what was originally the council estate at the top of Alcester Road – the route taken by Guide Friday until it was taken over by City Sightseeing. The war was over after five months of direct action.

If City Sightseeing had not withdrawn their buses from the disputed roads in Shottery I and Irena were prepared to up the ante again.

As far as we were concerned we were meeting threat with threat in defence of our peaceful way of life, which in the intervening years has made me think more about my kinsman Sean McDermott, the Irish rebel. He was meeting threat with threat too, in much more serious circumstances of course, and it cost him his life in the end. He was prepared to go that far in the total belief that what he was doing was the right thing to do.

The more I read about Sean, the more I recognise myself in my third cousin. Perhaps it took a violent childhood in Justin's Avenue to create forcibly the rebel in me, the bullied boy who grew tired of being knocked about, but the really rebellious trait, the potential hothead in me if you like, had always been in the DNA of the Keaneys. I'm now sure about that. I will always stand up for what I believe in and damn the consequences.

I think the whole family has heaved a huge sigh of relief I'm past it at last. Let's hope I am anyway.